FIRST EDITION
Building Bitcoin Websites

A Beginner's Guide to Bitcoin Focused Web Development

All rights reserved.
ISBN: 153494544X
ISBN-13: 978-1534945449

Written *By: Kyle Honeycutt*

Copyright © June 2016

*I'd like to dedicate this book to my wife,
Amber. Without her support and patience
this wouldn't have been possible.
I love you, Amber!*

Table of Contents:
1. Introduction 7
2. Bitcoin Basics 9
   2.1 What is Bitcoin?
   2.2 Bitcoin Addresses
   2.3 What is a Bitcoin?
   2.4 The Blockchain
   2.5 The Bitcoin Incentive
   2.6 Bitcoin Transaction Inputs and Outputs
   2.7 Bitcoin Terminology
3. Web Development Intro 21
   3.1 Text Editors
   3.2 Languages
   3.3 Services & Hosting
   3.4 Shared versus Dedicated Hosting
   3.5 Bitcoin Services
4. Hello Worlds 29
   4.1 HTML
   4.2 CSS
   4.3 JavaScript
   4.4 PHP Setup
   4.5 PHP
5. Your First Bitcoin Web App 47
   5.1 Getting the Exchange Rate
   5.2 File Get Contents and JSON Decode
   5.3 Write the Code
   5.4 Understanding the Output
6. Build a Bitcoin USD Converter App 53
   6.1 HTML Inputs
   6.2 JavaScript Functions
   6.3 onKeyUp and onChange
7. PROJECT: Build a Bitcoin Price Ticker Widget 61

    7.1 Where to start?
    7.2 HTML & CSS Framework
    7.3 Styling & Schematic
    7.4 More Styling
    7.5 PHP API Calls
    7.6 Getting The Data To Your Page
    7.7 Doing the Calculations
    7.8 Moving the PHP Values to HTML
    7.9 Make it Auto Refresh with JavaScript AJAX
8. 3rd Party APIs 81
    8.1 Overview
    8.2 Working with JSON data in PHP
    8.3 Blockchain.info API
    8.4 Receive Payments API
    8.5 Initiate the Request Using cURL
    8.6 Implementing the Callback
    8.7 Blockchain Wallet API
    8.8 Wallet API Setup
    8.9 VPS Setup
    8.10 Initiate Login
    8.11 Creating Addresses
    8.12 Sending Funds
9. Bitcoind JSON-RPC API 103
    9.1 Setup
    9.2 Config and Options
    9.3 Run and Test
    9.4 Your First JSON-RPC Calls
    9.5 Creating Addresses
    9.6 Sending Payments
    9.7 List of Commands
10. Databases and SQL 115
    10.1 Creating the Database
    10.2 Creating a Database Table

  10.3 Connecting to your Database with PHP
  10.4 Inserting Data
  10.5 Fetching Data
  10.6 Updating Data
  10.7 SQL Injection
11. Version Control – Git 131
  11.1 Download and Install Git
  11.2 Account Configuration
  11.3 Creating An Example GIT Project
  11.4 Committing a File
  11.5 Making Changes
12. PROJECT: Build a Basic E-Commerce Site (3rd party API) 141
  12.1 Layout and Build
  12.2 Create the Main Page
  12.3 Create the Product Pages
  12.4 Create the Checkout Page
  12.5 Creating the Payment Page
13. PROJECT: Build a Simple Game (JSON-RPC) 155
  13.1 Create the Database
  13.2 Create the Registration Page
  13.3 Create a Log In Page
  13.4 Creating the Game Page
  13.5 Building the Game Code
  13.6 Processing Deposits
  13.7 Allowing Withdrawals
  13.8 Adding Game Features

1. Introduction

The purpose of this book is to provide an introduction to web development with an emphasis on using the decentralized peer-to-peer cryptocurrency, Bitcoin. I am by no means an expert in the field, but rather an enthused hobbyist trying to guide others. As I began my adventure in early 2014 I noticed that there were a lot of tutorials for bitcoin mining, and using different exchanges, but none for bitcoin focused web development. The only resources available were scattered about the web with one-off questions from bewildered new-comers. Many inquiries would be left unanswered, or with multiple answers but no confirmed solution. Several others would end with a request for a payment in return for the answer. This translated into scavenger hunts that could take hours to find the answer to one simple question.

After a while I found myself doing the same scavenger hunts over and over again. I was surprised that there wasn't an existing resource with answers to the most common questions: *How do I fetch the current bitcoin price from an exchange? How can I generate new bitcoin addresses on my website for receiving payments? How do I send bitcoin with my website?*

In the latter-half of 2014 is when I decided I would start creating tutorials focused on building Bitcoin websites. I already had a bitcoin related domain lying around that I wasn't using so I started there by creating written tutorials. These pages would receive no views. I was experiencing what most beginning bloggers do, and that is the sense of writing to a non-existing audience. At this point I thought about giving up. No one was interested in my tutorials, so why should I spend so much time creating them? A real developer is bound to come around, and create tutorials a hundred times better than mine anyways, right? Well, good thing I didn't stop because now it's two years later, and I am still the only one creating Bitcoin focused web development tutorials.

Running a Bitcoin website is akin to opening a bank in the wild-west. You quickly become the target of thieves, and the only protection you have is your own; there is no intermediary that can stop or reverse a theft. This book is not a guide to creating a robust and un-hackable website, but instead a gentle guide on how to get started with building Bitcoin websites.

PRO TIP: You'll notice throughout this book next to code examples there will be numbers surrounded in curly brackets { }. This is a key to help you find the code on my Github incase you want to copy and paste a block of code.

Go to **github.com/coinables/Book** then locate the number that corresponds to the block of code you want to copy.

2. Bitcoin Basics

Before we leap into coding let's do a basic overview of Bitcoin the protocol. In order for you to start writing web applications that use bitcoin, you will need to understand the basics of how Bitcoin works. You might already notice, that sometimes I will refer to Bitcoin with a capital "B" and other times bitcoin with lower-case "b". When referring to Bitcoin the protocol I use a capital "B", and use lower-case "b" when referring to bitcoin the name of the currency unit.

For example, *"I sent John two bitcoins to cover the damage to his car"*, and *"My professor is teaching a class next year on Bitcoin"*.

2.1 What is Bitcoin?

There are entire books that try to answer this question. The best answer is we don't know yet, it is something that has never existed before so it is very difficult to explain to new comers because there is nothing to compare it to. Bitcoin is the first digital asset. This digital asset can be transferred to anyone with a Bitcoin address. It is not owned by anyone, it knows no borders, governments, political groups, race, sex, or class. Bitcoin is completely decentralized, and is open to anyone to use.

2.2 Bitcoin Addresses

Addresses are identifiers in the Bitcoin network that hold the claim to certain bitcoins. When bitcoins are sent to an address they can only be moved to another address by the one who owns the address.

Ownership of addresses are determined by who holds the private key that corresponds to the address, you can think of this similar to a password except it is 256 bits long (that's 256 1s and 0s). A private key can also be represented as 64 hexadecimal characters. Both of the above are raw examples of private keys, they still need to be converted into wallet import format (WIF) before they can be used by most wallet software.

So what's to keep two people from generating the same key? Nothing. Except gigantic numbers, a number that starts with 3 followed by 38 zeros. This number is so large the human mind cannot comprehend its vast space. Think of every atom in the universe, it's almost that big. If 7 billion people (nearly everyone on earth) started generating 1 million keys per second for 100 years that would only be 0.000000000006 of the total space. So you can rest assured as long as keys are generated randomly no two parties should ever generate a colliding key.

2.3 What is a Bitcoin?

Bitcoin itself is a protocol, and a bitcoin is the currency unit of value. When people think of digital items they think of files like an mp3 or jpg. There are no bitcoin files to represent the currency unit. The currency units are tracked by everyone in the Bitcoin network simultaneously using an open digital ledger known as the blockchain. A bitcoin can be divided down to eight decimal places making it very versatile for payments. There are no limits on who you can send bitcoin to or how much. You can send 10 cents or 10 million dollars.

2.4 The Blockchain

This is where things start to get technical, because to fully understand it you need to understand what hashing algorithms are and what they do.

On a basic level the blockchain is the name given to the public ledger that keeps track of every Bitcoin transaction. It is called the blockchain because approximately every ten minutes transactions are bundled into a batch of transactions called a block. This block is then linked back to the previous block using a hashing algorithm. At the time of this writing there are currently over 400,000 blocks, each one that is added gets linked back to the previous creating a chain.

Before one can add a block to the blockchain, it has to be validated by other users on the network. In order for it to be valid there must be a hash produced that fits a specific pattern. This is work done by computers known as proof of work. Proof of work keeps the blockchain secure. This is basically a process of elimination conducted by a computer at millions of attempts per second, this is what Bitcoin miners are doing. This prevents someone from arbitrarily adding blocks and creating a new longer chain. Due to the computational power required it is impossible for a single group, government or even multiple governments to rewrite the blockchain.

2.5 The Bitcoin Incentive

The same act that keeps the blockchain secure is how new bitcoins are created; this creates an incentive to keep the network strong and robust. Creating blocks needs to be difficult to mitigate attacks, but creating blocks needs to rewarded in order to create an incentive to keep the blockchain secure.

For every new block, the miner that discovers the correct hash is rewarded with 12.5 bitcoins. When Bitcoin first started the reward was 50, and then it was 25. It keeps halving every 210,000 blocks until 21 million coins have been issued. This is an important concept to keep in mind when you hear financial institutions or governments discussing creating their own blockchain. What keeps their blockchain secure? If it is proof of work, who will mine it? What is the incentive? If few will mine their blockchain it will not be secure, and if they have an insecure network the incentive they pay miners could lose value.

2.6 Bitcoin Transaction Inputs and Outputs

You will often hear Bitcoin described as a universal excel spreadsheet that keeps track of balances, but this is inaccurate. The blockchain keeps track of transaction inputs and outputs, balances are a byproduct manually calculated by wallets and block explorers.

The best way to explain this is with examples.

If Bob sends Alice 1 bitcoin, and Charles sends Alice 3 bitcoins then Alice will have 4 bitcions and 2 unspent outputs. If Alice then sends her 4 bitcoins and 2 unspent outputs to David, David will have 4 bitcoins and 1 unspent output.

Multiple inputs can be consolidated into a single output. Alternatively 1 input can be dispersed into multiple outputs.

Now let's go back to Alice having 4 bitcions and 2 unspent outputs. If David requests 3.1 bitcoins Alice will have to use both of her unspent outputs since the largest unspent output she has is only 3 bitcoins, but she will need to specify a change address if she wants that 0.9 difference back, if she does not specify an additional output for that 0.9 it will be automatically assumed as a miners fee.

People have lost a lot of money making this mistake in the past. Fortunately most modern wallets handle this automatically so you can transfer funds without ever having to think about change addresses.

To take it a little further let's imagine we have Elliott. Elliott doesn't have any money, so he tries to accumulate small amounts of bitcoins for free from faucets. After a month Elliott has earned 0.001 bitcoin, but since he received all small amounts separately there are 35 unspent outputs. At roughly 181 bytes per input this would create a transaction of 6kb, which is very large. Larger transactions require larger fees. The average fee is 0.0001 per kb, so Elliott's transaction would cost him 0.0006 in fees leaving only 0.0004 available to spend. If Elliott doesn't pay enough in fees his transaction can get held in limbo causing a large delay before the transaction is included in a block.

2.7 Bitcoin Terminology

Don't get scared by these new words. There's a lot of new terminology that a lot of people are unfamiliar with, and this part takes time and repetition.

For example the word 'hash', this word is used to describe so many different parts of Bitcoin including aspects of mining, individual transactions, public and private key generation… it can get really confusing to a new user. *I thought only bitcoin miners hashed. Addresses and transactions do hashing too?* Hash functions, or hashing is very popular in the cryptography space and its purpose is to take some arbitrary data of any length and produce a unique fixed length value that cannot be reversed.

```
An md5 hash of 'cow':
81566e986cf8cc685a05ac5b634af7f8

An md5 hash of 'man on the moon':
5b58693021fc45f4924b206cede66f0c
```

One of the most common purposes of hash functions is for password management. A website owner should store user's passwords as a hash instead of in plain text. This way if the web server is ever compromised the attacker will only end up with hashes instead of knowing what the users' actual passwords are. Now we could discuss the vulnerabilities of rainbow tables and the use of salts and HMAC, but that's a whole different topic.

Here are some other common Bitcoin terms you will come across:

- Blockchain – The Bitcoin blockchain is the distributed public ledger that keeps track of every transaction on the Bitcoin network. Everyone that runs the Bitcoin software will have a copy of the entire blockchain. If an attacker were to alter their copy of the blockchain their copy would be ignored because there are 6,000 other legitimate copies to compare it to. This is one of the reasons why Bitcoin is so secure.

- Mining – A computerized process of trial-and-error to match a pre-formatted output hash. Here's an example: I ask you to send me a SHA256 hash of your name but it must start with two zeros. A SHA256 hash of "Kyle" does not start with two zeros so you must add a salt(or nonce) until you get the desired output. The only way you could do this would be by trial-and-error, you can't not reverse solve for the nonce. A SHA256 hash of (Kyle+random_number) that starts with two zeros could take a while if you do it manually. Miners do a very similar thing but with transaction hashes instead of a name, and they have to solve for a lot more leading zeros. Even very poor performing miners are producing over a billion hashes (gigahash) per second. When a valid hash is found, the block is considered solved and the miner broadcasts it to the rest of the network. The miner is rewarded for solving the block, and the process starts over again.

- Block – Blocks are batches or a set of transactions that occur within a particular timeframe (roughly every ten minutes). All the transactions in the block are hashed and linked to the hash from the previous block, creating a chain, hence the name blockchain. If an attacker attempted to alter a transaction that occurred in the past it would produce a different hash for that block. Therefore all blocks after would also have a different hash. One tiny change to one transaction would result in an enormous change to the block hashes, making an attack like this stick out like a sore thumb. Additionally, the attacker would have to mine the altered block and all subsequent blocks before anyone on the network could mine one block. This becomes exponentially more difficult to accomplish the further in time the attempted alteration is.

- Proof of Work – POW or Proof of Work refers to the hashing power or energy that is required to mine a block. Since a valid block hash can only be found by trial-and-error, the act itself of finding a valid block hash is proof that the hashing work was performed.

- Address – Addresses are public hexadecimal strings that are used for receiving bitcoin. They are derived from a private-key that controls any unspent outputs assigned to the address. Anyone who possesses the private key to the address can spend the funds associated with that address.

- Private Key – You can think of this as a password. A private key is basically a 256 bit number. If you have 256 1s and 0s it can be converted into a Bitcoin private key, which can then be converted to a valid Bitcoin address. As long as you have access to the right algorithms you can create your own private key offline with dice, or by flipping a coin. Public/Private Key cryptography is not new. It's a mathematical way to prove that someone has possession of data without revealing that data to anyone else. One of the common uses is for signing SSL certificates (https).

- Wallet – Software or web service that stores Bitcoin keys, and assists the user with managing and creating transactions. Most wallets will add up the values of all the available unspent outputs, and display it as a "balance". This can be confusing to new users as you can only simultaneously create as many transactions as unspent outputs are available.

- Confirmations – When a transaction is broadcasted, it enters a queue to be included in a block. Transactions are not always included in the next block; sometimes, during a heavy level of transactions it might take a few blocks before the transaction finally gets included into a block. Once the transaction is included in the block it is considered to have one confirmation. Every subsequent block after will be an additional confirmation for the transaction. For example, if a transaction was initially included in block number 400,000 and the latest block that was mined is number 400,006 then this transaction now has six confirmations. Due to the proof of work that is required to mine blocks, the more confirmations that transaction has the more difficult it becomes to modify the transaction.

The best way to get familiar with Bitcoin is with hands-on experience. Get yourself a tiny bit of bitcoin, just a few dollars' worth so if you accidentally make a mistake it won't matter. Then practice sending bitcoin between addresses, creating private keys, and testing different wallets. Once you get a little experience with using Bitcoin everything should start making more sense.

The take away is Bitcoin is new, unique, and powerful. It makes it so that value can be as easy to store, send, and receive as an email. Bitcoin is its own protocol, and since it is still new it can be a bit tricky to integrate it with websites. There are few resources available currently for building on the HTTP protocol, and this book aims to be one of the first guides for beginning and intermediate web developers.

3. Web Development Intro & Organization

3.1 Text Editors

This is a rather boring topic, but it is your digital workstation. All the code that you will be writing and the majority of the time will be spent working with your text editor. So it is important to spend at least a little time discussing them.

Every Windows machine contains the notepad application. It is very simple but it can do everything you need to code an entire website in HTML, CSS, JavaScript, and PHP. Since it's just a basic text editor without any Rich Text Formatting(RTF) you can code just about anything using the basic notepad application. The downside is that it doesn't have any features that many coders find helpful, such as syntax highlighting, language detection, and auto-fills.

Notepad++ is a popular option for Windows users and personally my preferred text editor due to it being lightweight, open source, and its syntax highlighting features.

Sublime Text is another popular text editor that offers many features. It is not open-source.

Lime Text is an open source text editor created in GO and is considered a popular alternative to Sublime Text.

Brackets is a newer text editor from Adobe and surprisingly it is open source.

No matter which text editor you choose you will be able to follow along with this book. It's mainly a choice of preference, so try a few and see which one you like the best.

3.2 Languages

In this book we will be focusing on the LAMP stack. Linux, Apache, MySQL, PHP, Perl, and Python(LAMP). It is undoubtedly the most popular, free, and open-source stack for web development. If you already have a website or blog it is likely running on the LAMP stack! The vast majority of web hosts run the Linux operating system which then runs a version of the Apache web server. Don't worry you don't need to learn Linux or Apache to use the LAMP stack as most of this is already configured by your webhost. It is, however, good to learn to use Linux and Apache if you ever want to get more into the configuration and setup of your own personal web servers.

Personal Home Page(PHP) will be of heavy focus in this book. It will be our go-to language for developing applications, and interacting with the web server. PHP is often considered one of the most popular, and easiest to learn server-side scripting languages. PHP is very powerful, and is responsible for running a wide array of websites from small personal blogs, to message board forums, to social media sites.

HyperText Markup Language(HTML) is a very simple yet essential language for front-end development of a website. HTML is responsible for elements that are visible to a user on a page. Text, images, checkboxes, input forms, and buttons are all done in HTML. HTML also holds very important meta data about a website that makes it searchable by search engine robots.

Cascading Style Sheets(CSS) is an easy to understand, but difficult to master styling scripting language. CSS can be hard-coded into the `<head>` of an HTML page or it can be stored externally as a separate .css file. Doing so makes it easy to change the look of an entire website by altering a single source of code from the main .css file instead of having to change every page individually.

JavaScript, not to be confused with Java, is a front-end scripting language that adds interactivity and processing to a webpage. JavaScript can be used to create a simple game, calculate figures on a form, animate elements, and much more. It is no surprise that this language has evolved into much more than just a front-end language. A new stack has emerged known as the MEAN stack. MongoDB, ExpressJS, AngularJS, and NodeJS(MEAN) allows coding with JavaScript syntax nearly throughout the entire stack.

Front-end languages are run on the client (website viewer) side, and back-end or server-side languages are ran on the web server (website owner) side. Server-side languages are private and as long as the code is secure it cannot be manipulated or viewed by a visitor. Front-end languages should be treated like public access as any viewer can easily view the code and even manipulate the way it runs.

A developer could create a login form with just JavaScript with passwords stored in a .js file, but this can be easily circumvented by viewing the page source or manipulated using built-in browser developer tools. The proper way to handle a login form is by storing the hashed passwords in a MySQL database and then use a server-side scripting language such as PHP, Python, NodeJS, etc to handle the verification and login process.

Once you get started with JavaScript and PHP you will begin to notice similarities between them and other programming languages. With practice wit will become easier to learn other programming languages as you will notice syntax and structure is similar to what you already know.

3.3 Services and Hosting

This section will be very brief as I am not making recommendations or going over every possible service. I do however want to go over them since most of us will not be running home-based web servers.

As a web developer you will mainly be working with two different types of services. A domain provider and a web host provider. Most of these services have merged into one in the same, so you use one provider that will handle both domain name server and the web hosting service.

Domain Name Servers handle the .com, .net, .org, etc for your website's IP address. On a very basic level it makes accessing websites easier. Instead of typing in 173.194.199.99, which is difficult to remember, you can just enter google.com.

Web Host Providers store the files and run the actual server that your site runs on. When running server-side languages like PHP you will need a web server to execute the files. PHP files will not run on your own home computer unless you install Apache and PHP on your computer.

If you are interested in testing PHP files on your computer look into programs like XAMPP, WAMP, or something of that nature. I often utilize sites like phpfiddle.org and codepad.org when testing snippets of my code.

If you are looking to follow along with this book, but you do not want to register a domain name or pay for hosting your best option is using a program like XAMPP. This will allow you to run your website from your own computer for your own personal viewing. It will not be broadcasted out to the world unless you modify your home router to forward the correct port (usually port 80) which is not recommended.

3.4 Shared versus Dedicated Hosting

When you are picking out your hosting some will be shared and some will be dedicated or Virtual Private Servers(VPS). Shared hosting runs your site and other websites from the same server. Since it is shared with others you will not have root access to the server which could limit you from running certain services like nodeJS. Dedicated and VPS hosting gives your site its own virtual server where you have root access and allows you to make nearly any change you would like.

Dedicated hosting typically comes with a higher cost than shared hosting. I recommend you become familiar with using shared hosting and Linux command lines before using a VPS.

3.5 Bitcoin Services

Since this is still a new and emerging market this part will be difficult to cover. Many services come and go quickly or they frequently change terms, services, and features. The good thing about the competitive ecosystem is that a lot of services are open source, and have free APIs available. The bad thing is most of this section will be out-dated just a few months after publishing.

Coinbase – Probably the best known source to buy and sell bitcoin in the United States. Operating since 2012 they have gained a lot of trust from both the Bitcoin community and government regulators. Since they have to play on both sides of the fence to keep their business legal, they are often criticized for their compliance of Know Your Customer/Anti-Money Laundering(KYC/AML). Coinbase offers an API to registered merchants to make accepting bitcoin payments easier. A formal application process is required to use their merchant API. In 2014 Coinbase launched Toshi a free public API to query blockchain data, addresses, and transactions. In 2015 they launched a regulated and licensed exchange.

Blockchain.info – A well-known block explorer that has been running since 2011. They provide free personal wallet services (web and mobile), blockchain data API, and free merchant APIs. They do not have a formal application process to open a wallet or use their API services.

Bitpay – A popular choice for merchants looking to accept bitcoin. They require an application process to use their merchant services.

Mycelium – A well respected mobile wallet. In 2015 they ventured into the payment processing sector with their release of Gear. Mycelium Gear makes it easy to create a "buy now" type of widget for websites, as well as, a free developer API. They do not require an application process to use their services.

There are many other services that I have not mentioned. Be careful whenever dealing with a new service. The amount of scams in the Bitcoin world is high, so it's best to remain very skeptical.

4. Hello Worlds

This is the part of the book where the programming begins! I debated whether or not I wanted this book to jump right into coding, but I decided to go with a few introduction chapters since this book's focus is on web development in multiple languages and Bitcoin. Considering this we are going to do multiple Hello World's.

Nearly every book in the programming space will have a "Hello World" where you create your first program that outputs the words "Hello World". The great thing about a Hello World is that it's a starting point that anyone can follow along and reproduce with the same result. No experience required!

Hello World – HTML, CSS, JavaScript, & PHP

This is going to be a crash course into HTML, CSS, JavaScript, and PHP. By the end of this chapter you will have written a single web page that uses all four languages.

4.1 HTML

HTML is the basic building block language for the web, making this language the best fit for our first exercise.

Begin by opening your text editor of choice; we went over different text editors in Chapter 3.

Create a new blank file if your text editor does not do so automatically.

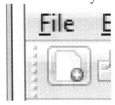

Now you should have a blank page. Only two steps left open and close the HTML tags and then enter the text. You can think of the HTML tags like a cover on a book there is one to start and another to end. Everything else in between is the content. The HTML syntax is consistent where elements are always held within < > symbols.

Let's now open our HTML tags.

```
<html>
```

Closing tags is just as simple, except it includes a / at the beginning.

```
</html>
```

In between your HTML tags we will type Hello World!

```
Hello World!
```

Your file should now look like this:

{101}
```
<html>
Hello World!
</html>
```

That's it you just coded your first web page! Now we just need to save it and run it in a browser.

Go to File -> Save As

Save the file to your desktop, select the file type as Hyper Text Markup Language, and name the file.

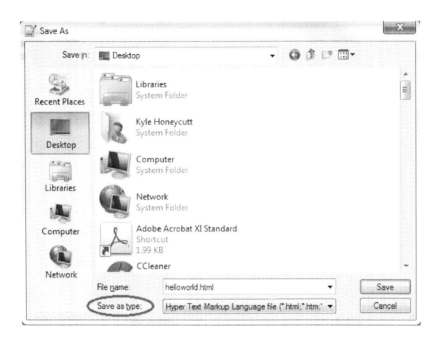

Navigate to your desktop and open the file you just created. It should automatically open up in your default web browser.

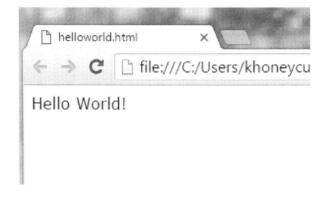

What we created is a very basic bare-bones HTML page. Now let's add a few more HTML tags. Let's add <!DOCTYPE html>, <head>, and <body>. These tags will not produce much of a visual change since these are structure tags. DOCTYPE tells the browser what version of HTML we are running, HEAD will hold meta, style, and other background data, and BODY will hold the majority of our visible content to users.

{102}
```
<!DOCTYPE html>
<html>
<head>
</head>
<body>
Hello World!
</body>
</html>
```

Now let's add inside our HEAD tags. The <title> tag will allow us to change what is displayed on the browser tab. Since we currently do not have a TITLE tag the browser tab displays the file name "helloworld.html". Let's change that to read "Hello World!". Remember this will go inside the HEAD tags.

{103}
```
<!DOCTYPE html>
<html>
<head>
<title>Hello World!</title>
</head>
<body>
Hello World!
</body>
</html>
```

PRO TIP: The TITLE tag is also frequently indexed by search engines crawlers. Many times top ranking sites will have your search phrase in the TITLE tags. A title of "How to trade bitcoin" is more SEO friendly than "Jim's Bitcoin Trading Blog".

Our HEAD tags will also include important meta data that provide search engines information about your site. `<meta name="Description" content="Learn to trade bitcoin with Jim">` can provide search engines with a short description of your website. With the emergence of social networking and link sharing the more popular Open Graph(OG) meta-tags have become. `<meta property="og:title" content="How to trade bitcoin">` Do a web search on Open Graph Meta Tags if you want a list of different properties available.

4.2 CSS

The next HEAD tag we are going to use will lead us into our next language CSS. Add in `<style>` tags and inside of them we will change the background-color and the font style.

{104}
```
<style>
html,body {
   background-color: #cccccc;
   font-family: sans-serif;
}
</style>
```

The first part sets the target of what we want to style. The properties of our style for that target must be within curly braces { }, and each property within the curly braces must end with a semi-colon.

The color I selected is a light gray, and is defined in hexadecimal (0-9, A-F). Want to use a different color? Do a web search on hexadecimal colors and you will find endless resources.

Here's what we have now:

{105}
```
<!DOCTYPE html>
<html>
<head>
<title>Hello World!</title>
<meta name="Description" content="To the Moon!">
<style>
html,body{
  background-color: #cccccc;
  font-family: sans-serif;
}
</style>
</head>
<body>
Hello World!
</body>
</html>
```

Save and run:

CSS styling can be very simple like what we just did, or very complex. Advanced CSS users can create complex shapes and simple images using nothing but CSS code. In this book I am going to stick with basic CSS styling. Next, we are going to create an element, and then target a specific element in CSS.

Navigate back to the `<body>` tags and we are going to change our content slightly. Open and close some `<div>` tags, and inside write "Hello Bitcoin!".

```
<div>Hello Bitcoin!</div>
```

We can now target the DIV tag in our CSS, and change the font color to orange. Note that CSS will also recognize colors based on color name.

```
div{
    color: orange;
}
```

Since the DIV is within the HTML and BODY tags it will inherit the properties of background-color and font-family.

{106}
```
<!DOCTYPE html>
<html>
<head>
<title>Hello World!</title>
<meta name="Description" content="To the Moon!">
<style>
html,body{
  background-color: #cccccc;
  font-family: sans-serif;
}
div{
  color: orange;
}
</style>
</head>
<body>
Hello World!
<div>Hello Bitcoin!</div>
</body>
```

```
</html>
```

Save and run:

Giving a tag a style like we did with DIV will affect all `<div>` tags on a page. Most pages will have more than one `<div>`, so we will need to clarify which ones we want to target. We can do this using class and identification properties.

Let's add `<div>` tags to our existing "Hello World!"

```
<div>Hello World!</div>
```

Also let's add an identification property to the "Hello Bitcoin!" DIV.

```
<div id="bc">Hello Bitcoin!</div>
```

Now both DIVs will be the color orange since they are within `<div>` tags, but we can now specifically style the "Hello Bitcoin!" `<div>` since we gave it an id property. We can target id properties in CSS by using # (number sign, pound, hashtag). Alternatively, target classes using . (period).

In the `<style>` tags, add to our existing style targeting the bc identification property `#bc`, then we'll make the font bold and give it border.

```
    #bc{
        font-weight: bold;
        border: 2px solid #333333;
    }
```

Now we have:

{107}
```
<!DOCTYPE html>
<html>
<head>
<title>Hello World!</title>
<meta name="Description" content="To the Moon!">
<style>
html,body{
  background-color: #cccccc;
  font-family: sans-serif;
}
div{
  color: orange;
}
#bc{
  font-weight: bold;
  border: 2px solid #333333;
}
</style>
</head>
<body>
Hello World!
<div id="bc">Hello Bitcoin!</div>
</body>
</html>
```

Save and run:

A class is intended to be used when you have multiple elements that you want to style the same way. Identification properties are for unique elements. To further clarify, you should never have more than one DIV with the same id property, but you can have several DIVs that share the same class.

CSS code does not have to be within <style> tags for every page. If you have a website with 200 pages, and you decided you wanted to change your color scheme, you would have to update every single page. This would be a huge waste of time. We can create a separate CSS file and then reference it once in our <head> tags. This way you can update all pages just by changing the main CSS file.

Start by creating a new file.

Copy all of your <style> code from the page we have been working on and paste it into the new file. Remove the <style> tags so you are only left with the CSS code.

```
1   html,body {
2       background-color: #cccccc;
3       font-family: sans-serif;
4   }
5   div{
6       color: orange;
7   }
8   #bc{
9       font-weight: bold;
10      border: 2px solid #333333;
11  }
12
```

Now save the file as a .css file type.

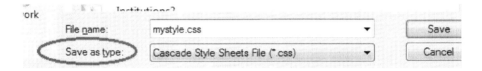

Now that we have our style saved on another file, we will need to tell our HTML page to fetch that file. Back on our HTML file, within our <head> tags replace where we had our style code with:

```
<link rel="stylesheet" type="text/css" href="mystyle.css">
```

Once you have that done, it should look like:

{108}
```
<!DOCTYPE html>
<html>
<head>
<title>Hello World!</title>
<meta name="Description" content="To the Moon!">
```

```
<link rel="stylesheet" type="text/css" href="mystyle.css">
</head>
<body>
Hello World!
<div id="bc">Hello Bitcoin!</div>
</body>
</html>
```

Now let's transition over to some JavaScript.

4.3 JavaScript

In our HTML body let's create a new DIV under our two existing with an id property of "js".

```
<div id="js"></div>
```

Now let's add some `<script>` tags that will add some text to the DIV we just created.

{109}
```
<script>
document.getElementById("js").innerHTML = "Hello Javascript!";
</script>
```

Notice how we targeted the DIV using id property, like we did with CSS. You should have:

{110}
```
<!DOCTYPE html>
<html>
<head>
<title>Hello World!</title>
<meta name="Description" content="To the Moon!">
<link rel="stylesheet" type="text/css" href="mystyle.css">
</head>
<body>
Hello World!
<div id="bc">Hello Bitcoin!</div>
<div id="js"></div>
<script>
document.getElementById("js").innerHTML = "Hello Javascript!";
</script>
```

```
</body>
</html>
```

Save and run:

Well that was boring! Let's add a tiny bit of interactivity, since one of the most popular uses for JavaScript is interactivity. In our HTML we'll add `<button>` tags and write "Click Me!" in between the tags to label the button.

```
<button>Click Me!</button>
```

Let's wrap our existing JavaScript with a function, so that we can tell it when to execute.

{111}
```
function jsButton() {
document.getElementById("js").innerHTML = "Hello JavaScript!";
}
```

Lastly we need to tell the button what to do. We will use the `onClick` listener to run our jsButton function when the button is clicked. Edit your existing `<button>` tags to include a `onClick="jsButton();"`

{112}
```
<button onClick="jsButton();">Click Me!</button>
```

Put it all together and we have:

{113}
```
<!DOCTYPE html>
<html>
<head>
<title>Hello World!</title>
<meta name="Description" content="To the Moon!">
<link rel="stylesheet" type="text/css" href="mystyle.css">
</head>
<body>
Hello World!
<div id="bc">Hello Bitcoin!</div>
<div id="js"></div>
<button onClick="jsButton();">Click Me!</button>
<script>
function jsButton(){
document.getElementById("js").innerHTML = "Hello Javascript!";
}
</script>
</body>
</html>
```

Save and run:

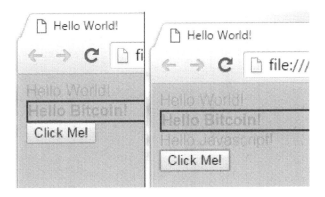

4.4 PHP Setup

So far we have hit HTML, CSS, and JavaScript. Before we can start with PHP we will need to set ourselves up to be able to run PHP files. *If you already have a web server running you will be able to run PHP files fine.*

XAMPP is a free and open source platform that lets you run a web server on your computer. Once installed and running you will be able to run PHP files on your computer.

At the time of this writing, XAMPP can be downloaded from https://www.apachefriends.org.

Download XAMPP and follow the installation instructions.

Once installed, launch the application and run/activate the Apache server. Any PHP file you add the htdocs directory, typically `C:/xampp/htdocs` can now be ran through your browser under `localhost`. For example, let's say you have a php file named `myfile.php`, and save it to your `xampp/htdocs` directory. You can now access it by directing your browser to `localhost/myfile.php`.

Now that we can run PHP files on our computer let's do our PHP Hello World.

4.5 PHP

Before we can start writing our code we need to tell our web server we are writing in PHP. Do this by using our open and close PHP tags.

Open:
```
<?php
```
Close:
```
?>
```

Anything written in between the open and close tags will be interpreted by the server as PHP. PHP code is a server-side language and can only be viewed by the server, whereas HTML, CSS, and JavaScript code can be viewed by anyone visiting the website.

Underneath our JavaScript button we'll use the `echo` command to print "Hello PHP" on the screen in PHP.

```
<?php echo "Hello PHP!"; ?>
```

{114}
```
<!DOCTYPE html>
<html>
<head>
<title>Hello World!</title>
<meta name="Description" content="To the Moon!">
<link rel="stylesheet" type="text/css" href="mystyle.css">
</head>
<body>
Hello World!
<div id="bc">Hello Bitcoin!</div>
<div id="js"></div>
<button onClick="jsButton();">Click Me!</button>
<br>
<?php echo "Hello PHP!"; ?>
<script>
function jsButton(){
document.getElementById("js").innerHTML = "Hello Javascript!";
}
</script>
</body>
</html>
```

Congratulations! You just completed a Hello World crash course in HTML, CSS, JavaScript, and PHP! This is basically all the languages you need to start building professional web applications, in exception of MySQL which we will cover later. In the next chapter we will create our first working Bitcoin application.

5. Your First Bitcoin Web App

In our last chapter we started with HTML then made our way to PHP. For building our web app we are going to start with PHP and work backwards. Although it might sound complicated what we will be doing is very simple. We are going to use PHP to fetch the current exchange rate from an exchange, and then use HTML and CSS to display it on our website. Very simple!

5.1 Getting the Exchange Rate

Since bitcoin is traded on the open market there are multiple exchanges. Every exchange will have a different exchange rate for the value of a bitcoin. So your first step will be deciding which exchange you want to get your exchange rate from. I prefer to use popular exchanges to get the most accurate rate.

Btc-e, one of the oldest exchanges, is a good place to start because their API is public (no sign-up) and easy to use.

To locate the public API end-point for btc-e just do a simple web search for "btc-e api ticker". At the time of this writing, their USD exchange rate URL is at (https://btc-e.com/api/3/ticker/btc_usd).

If you visit this URL in a browser you should see something like:

```
{"btc_usd":
{"high":417.569,"low":408,"avg":412.7845,"vol":2692899
.50125,"vol_cur":6535.15727,"last":413.891,"buy":413.8
9,"sell":413.831,"updated":1457553866}}
```

This is a JavaScript Object Notation (JSON) formatted response. JSON format is easily interpreted by most programming languages, which is why it is widely used with APIs.

5.2 File Get Contents and JSON Decode

To get the exchange rate we will have to reach out to an external resource (in this case btc-e), capture the information we want, and return it to our server. To do so we will be using the PHP command `file_get_contents();`. This command basically tells PHP that we need to go somewhere else to get information.

We will also need to tell PHP that the data we are fetching is in JSON format. By using the command `json_decode();` it will translate the JSON into a PHP associative array making it easier for PHP to handle.

All that is left is for us to write the code using the information we just went over.

5.3 Write the Code

Start by setting the exchange rate URL to a variable. Variables always start with a dollar-sign `$` and you can name them how you wish.

```
$url = "https://btc-e.com/api/3/ticker/btc_usd";
```

Now the exchange rate URL is stored under `$url` and we can plug it into the `file_get_contents();` command.

```
file_get_contents($url);
```

That's great, but we also needed to tell it to translate or decode the JSON. Give the `file_get_contents();` a variable so we can plug it into a `json_decode();`. Also give the `json_decode();` a variable name.

{115}
```
$url = "https://btc-e.com/api/3/ticker/btc_usd";
$fileGet = file_get_contents($url);
$json = json_decode($fileGet, TRUE);
```

At this point we can see if we have successfully fetched this information by dumping the variable `$json` using `var_dump();`.

```
var_dump($json);
```

All together you should have:

{116}
```php
<?php
$url = "https://btc-e.com/api/3/ticker/btc_usd";
$fileGet = file_get_contents($url);
$json = json_decode($fileGet, TRUE);
var_dump($json);
?>
```

5.4 Understanding the Output

Save your PHP file and run it. You should see the same information you saw when you visited the URL (https://btc-e.com/api/3/ticker/btc_usd) but instead of JSON format it will be broken down into an associative array.

```
array(1)
  {
  ["btc_usd"]=> array(9)
     {
     ["high"]=> float(417.569)
     ["low"]=> int(408)
     ["avg"]=> float(412.7845)
     ["vol"]=> float(2760608.39007)
     ["vol_cur"]=> float(6698.34972)
     ["last"]=> float(412.951)
     ["buy"]=> float(412.951)
     ["sell"]=> float(412.653)
     ["updated"]=> int(1457558209)
     }
  }
```

This is actually a multi-dimensional array because we have an array within an array. The only value within the initial array is "btc_usd". The "btc_usd" value holds another array that contains nine values. So in order to access any of the data that we are after such as "avg", we will have to access "btc_usd" first.

Go back to your line with the `var_dump` and replace it with the following.

```
echo $json["btc_usd"]["last"];
```

Save your PHP file and run it, and it should display the most recent exchange rate.

Now you can add whatever you would like to make it yours. Add a bitcoin graphic, include a dollar sign, or change the style and colors. Once you make any final changes you have completed your first bitcoin web app. The next chapter we are going to add a little bit of interactivity using JavaScript!

{117}
```
<?php
$url = "https://btc-e.com/api/3/ticker/btc_usd";
$fileGet = file_get_contents($url);
$json = json_decode($fileGet, TRUE);
?>
<!DOCTYPE html>
<html>
<head>
<title>My First Web App</title>
<style>
#container{
   font-size: 40px;
   font-family: sans-serif;
   text-align: center;
}
</style>
</head>
<body>
<div id="container">
   <img src="bitcoin.jpg"><br>
```

```
    $<?php echo $json["btc_usd"]["last"]; ?>
</div>
</body>
</html>
```

$416.483

PRO TIP: Did you know the Bitcoin logo font is Ubuntu Bold Italic? You can import to your webpage free using Google web fonts.

{118}
```
<link href='https://fonts.googleapis.com/css?family=Ubuntu:700italic' rel='stylesheet' type='text/css'>
```

Then just integrate it into your CSS by calling 'Ubuntu':

```
font-family: 'Ubuntu', sans-serif;
```

6. Build a Bitcoin USD Converter App

Our last chapter we created our first bitcoin web application where it grabbed the current exchange rate, and displayed it on the screen. We are going to build off our last chapter and build a simple currency converter. The converter will take an input of bitcoin or USD value, and then convert the corresponding value using JavaScript.

A converter needs to work both ways. If a user enters in 20 dollars we need it to convert to the amount of bitcoin required to be equal to 20 US Dollars, alternatively if they enter 0.4 BTC we need it to convert to the US Dollar equivalent. To do this we will be creating two JavaScript functions.

6.1 HTML Inputs

Inside our body tags within our HTML we are going to create two input boxes using the `<input>` tags, each will need their own identifier property and a type property of text.

{119}
```
<input type="text" id="btc">
<input type="text" id="usd">
```

The default input box looks like this:

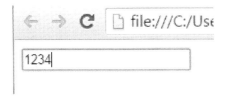

You can leave it how it is or you can style the input boxes using CSS.

The above example in CSS is:

{120}
```
#btc{
    width: 150px;
    height: 40px;
    border: 2px solid #333;
    border-radius: 5px;
    font-size: 22px;
    font-family: sans-serif;
}
```

Now that we have our input boxes let's write our JavaScript.

6.2 JavaScript Functions

Below our input boxes open and close your `<script>` tags. Create a variable named btc, and have it be equal to the PHP `echo` of last price from our last chapter.

{121}
```
<script>
var btc = <?php echo $json["btc_usd"]["last"]; ?>;
</script>
```

This will store the latest bitcoin price under the variable "btc".

Create a function and give it a name of whatever you like, I will be using "btcConvert".

{122}
```
function btcConvert(){
};
```

Before we can make the conversion calculation we need to know what value the user entered into our "btc" input box. We can grab this value using `getElementById()`; which uses the identification properties to target a piece of HTML code. Since we have an identification property of "btc" set to our input box we will enter "btc" within the parentheses. We'll then use the `.value` attribute to get the value of the "btc" input box and assign it to a variable named "amount".

{123}
```
var amount = document.getElementById("btc").value;
```

With the variable "amount" holding the users input, and "btc" holding the current value of one bitcoin we can use simple math to make the conversion.

Multiply "amount" with "btc", and assign it to a new variable named "btcCalc".

```
var btcCalc = amount * btc;
```

We can then update the "btcCalc" variable to only show two decimal places using the `toFixed()` function.

{124}
```
var btcCalc = btcCalc.toFixed(2);
```

Our function is almost complete. We need to tell JavaScript to fill the other input box with our end result calculation. We can also do this using the `getElementById();` function we used earlier, but this time we want to target our "usd" input box.

{125}
```
document.getElementById("usd").value = btcCalc;
```

The completed function should now look like this:

{126}
```
function btcConvert(){
  var amount = document.getElementById("btc").value;
  var btcCalc = amount * btc;
  var btcCalc = btcCalc.toFixed(2);
  document.getElementById("usd").value = btcCalc;
};
```

We will now create a second function but reverse the process. Get the value of "usd" first, then divide "usd" from "btc" and send the output to the "btc" input box. Name this new function usdConvert.

{127}
```
function usdConvert(){
 var usd = document.getElementById("usd").value;
 var usdCalc =  usd / btc;
 var usdCalc = usdCalc.toFixed(8);
 document.getElementById("btc").value = usdCalc;
}
```

You'll notice I also changed the `toFixed()` from two to eight, since the bitcoin currency unit has eight decimal places.

Our JavaScript section is now complete.

{128}
```
<script>
var btc = <?php echo $json["btc_usd"]["last"]; ?>;
function btcConvert(){
 var amount = document.getElementById("btc").value;
 var btcCalc = amount * btc;
 var btcCalc = btcCalc.toFixed(2);
 document.getElementById("usd").value = btcCalc;
};

function usdConvert(){
 var usd = document.getElementById("usd").value;
 var usdCalc =  usd / btc;
 var usdCalc = usdCalc.toFixed(8);
 document.getElementById("btc").value = usdCalc;
}
</script>
```

6.3 onKeyUp and onChange

We're almost done we just need to tell our page when to run the two functions we just created.

Back in our `<input>` tags we are going to use the `onChange` and `onKeyUp` attributes to trigger our two functions.

The onKeyUp attribute will respond after a keyboard-key is pressed and released.

The onChange attribute will respond whenever there is a change made to the element. Since we already have the onKeyUp why do we need the onChange? The onChange will also react if a user pastes in a value with their mouse -> right-click -> paste.

Inside our "btc" input box set the onChange and onKeyUp equal to our btcConvert(); function.

{129}
```
<input type="text" id="btc" onchange="btcConvert();" onkeyup="btcConvert();">
```

Then set the "usd" input box to call the usdConvert(); function.

{130}
```
<input type="text" id="usd" onchange="usdConvert();" onkeyup="usdConvert();">
```

That's it! Save and run your PHP file, and you will have a functioning bitcoin/US Dollar conversion web app.

{131}
```php
<?php
$url = "https://btc-e.com/api/3/ticker/btc_usd";
$fileGet = file_get_contents($url);
$json = json_decode($fileGet, TRUE);
?>
<!DOCTYPE html>
<html>
<head>
<title>My First Web App</title>
<style>
#container{
    font-size: 40px;
    font-family: sans-serif;
    text-align: center;
}
#btc, #usd{
      width: 175px;
      height: 40px;
      border: 2px solid #333;
      border-radius: 5px;
      font-size: 22px;
      font-family: sans-serif;
}
</style>
</head>
<body>
<div id="container">
   <img src="bitcoin.jpg"><br>
   <input type="text" id="btc" onchange="btcConvert();" onkeyup="btcConvert();">
   <input type="text" id="usd" onchange="usdConvert();" onkeyup="usdConvert();">
</div>
<script>
```

```
var btc = <?php echo $json["btc_usd"]["last"]; ?>;

function btcConvert(){
 var amount = document.getElementById("btc").value;
 var btcCalc = amount * btc;
 var btcCalc = btcCalc.toFixed(2);
 document.getElementById("usd").value = btcCalc;
};

function usdConvert(){
 var usd = document.getElementById("usd").value;
 var usdCalc =  usd / btc;
 var usdCalc = usdCalc.toFixed(8);
 document.getElementById("btc").value = usdCalc;
}
</script>
</body>
</html>
```

7. PROJECT: Build a Bitcoin Price Ticker Widget

This chapter we are going to build a simple bitcoin price ticker widget. It will display the current or last price, as well as some historical data. To create the widget we will use HTML, CSS, JavaScript and PHP.

Here's an example of the end result:

Requirements:
1. Web server with PHP

7.1 Where to start?

When working on web projects and you handle everything from concept to deployment, you might find yourself wondering where to start.

This part is really up to you. I like to start with what I think will be the most tricky so I can plan everything else based on how the tricky part turns out. If you have never tried cronjobs or sqlite before you might want to start there to make sure you don't have any issues. These are just examples, we won't actually be using cronjobs or sqlite in this project.

For this tutorial we will begin with the layout and design, and then work our way to the back-end.

7.2 HTML & CSS Framework

Begin by building out your basic page framework with HTML, head, body, style tags.

{132}
```
<!DOCTYPE html>
<html>
<head>
<title>My BTC Widget</title>
<style>
</style>
</head>
<body>
</body>
</html>
```

7.3 Styling & Schematic

Add in a DIV that will be our main container to hold the widget. Give it an ID of "container".

In our CSS we will define the dimensions, make it so that if any code within the DIV extends outside of the container it will be hidden. Round-off our border, and set the colors.

{133}
```
<style>
#container{
    width: 275px;
    height: 90px;
    overflow: hidden;
    background-color: #2f2f2f;
    border: 1px solid #000;
    border-radius: 5px;
    color: #fefdfb;
}
</style>
</head>
<body>
<div id="container">
</div>
</body>
```

Add a table inside the DIV with 2 columns and 4 rows. The first cell will have a rowspan of 3 and the last cell will have a colspan of 2. And let's fill in the cells with some templated data.

Table schematic

{last price}	{% change}
	{HIGH}
	{LOW}
	{DATE & TIME}

{133a}
```
<div id="container">
<table width="100%">
<tr>
        <td rowspan="3" width="60%">
        {last price}
        </td>
        <td align="right">
        {change}
        </td>
</tr>
        <td align="right">
        {high}
        </td>
<tr>
        <td align="right">
        {low}
        </td>
</tr>
<tr>
        <td align="right" colspan="2">
        {date & time}
        </td>
</tr>
</table>
</div>
```

You should now have something that looks like this:

```
                        {change}
{last price}            {high}
                        {low}
                        {date & time}
```

7.4 More Styling

A few changes we want to make at this time.

The {last price} should stand out the most, so let's make it's font bold and larger.

Also {date & time} is less significant but nice to have, so let's make is smaller and change the color to make it stand out less.

Give the <td> that holds last price an ID of "lastPrice", and the <td> that holds the date an ID of "dateTime".

{134}
```
<tr>
        <td rowspan="3" width="60%" id="lastPrice">
        {last price}
        </td>
        <td align="right">
        {change}
        </td>
</tr>
        <td align="right">
        {high}
        </td>
<tr>
        <td align="right">
        {low}
        </td>
</tr>
<tr>
        <td align="right" colspan="2" id="dateTime">
        {date & time}
        </td>
</tr>
```

Now update the CSS to modify these two cells so that last price is larger and date and time is smaller.

{135}
```
#lastPrice{
        font-size: 24px;
        font-weight: bold;
}
#dateTime{
        font-size: 9px;
        color: #999;
}
```

Now we have this:

Great! The templating is done and now we can use an exchange API to fill in our data.

7.5 PHP API Calls

Bitstamp offers a free public API that allows up to 600 requests per hour (once per second). If your server exceeds this limit Bitstamp will ban your IP. Our script will refresh every 15 seconds so this will leave a large buffer from us hitting the limit. Consider multiple users using your widget at one time so you don't want to hit it once per second. Every 15 seconds should create enough of a buffer that even if your widget receives moderate usage you should not exceed the limits. Since Bitstamp's cutoff is based on requests per hour, it would require 600 users within one hour to exceed the limit. This is unlikely, since most users will only be accessing your widget for a few minutes each, not a full hour, while they read whatever page they are on.

PRO TIP: I prefer to store these values in a database and have an automated task update the values every N minutes. This means I will never exceed the limits since users will be querying my own database instead of Bitstamp and page loads will be much faster. Also we could use websocket instead but I'm not going to cover that in this tutorial since I want to keep this relatively simple.

Head on over to https://www.bitstamp.net/api/ticker/

You should see a JSON array of data that looks something like this:

```
{"high": "415.22", "last": "413.32000000", "timestamp":
"1457982915", "bid": "413.15000000", "vwap": "413.28",
"volume": "4128.31330337", "low": "410.50", "ask":
"413.32000000", "open": 412.99}
```

This single API end-point will provide us with every category we need except for the 24 hour change percentage. For that we will have to calculate it manually using the "open" value. Since Bitcoin markets are always open, the "open" is actually just the price 24 hours ago making the 24 hour change percentage easy to calculate.

7.6 Getting The Data To Your Page

Okay so we've found the API end-point and the data we need, but how do we get it on our page? The answer is PHP. PHP will allow us to grab that information, parse the JSON data and display it on our page.

Begin by opening your PHP tags at the very top of your document, before `<!DOCTYPE html>`

Open:
```
<?php
```
Close:
```
?>
```

67

Anything you type between these tags will be interpreted as PHP.

Now let's create a variable and make it equal to the Bitstamp URL from earlier

```
$url = "https://www.bitstamp.net/api/ticker/";
```

We can then tell PHP to fetch that page using a prebuilt PHP function called `file_get_contents()`

```
$fgc = file_get_contents($url);
```

Then we need to tell PHP to read it as JSON, `json_decode()` will turn the JSON data into a PHP array to make it easier to work with.

```
$json = json_decode($fgc, TRUE);
```

Great, now we can pull the data we using the `$json` variable.

{136}
```
<?php
$url = "https://www.bitstamp.net/api/ticker/";
$fgc = file_get_contents($url);
$json = json_decode($fgc, TRUE);
$lastPrice = $json["last"];
$highPrice = $json["high"];
$lowPrice = $json["low"];
?>

<!DOCTYPE html>
```

Now the `$lastPrice` variable holds the latest price, `$highPrice` holds the high price, and so on.

One problem we have is that the last price feed from Bistamp, has eight decimal places, and we only want to display two. We can trim off the extra decimals using `number_format();`

Example without number_format
```
$lastPrice;
echo lastPrice;
//will output 413.32000000
```
Example with number_format
```
$lastPrice = number_format($lastPrice, 2);
echo $lastPrice;
//will output 413.32
```

7.7 Doing the Calculations

Now we can calculate the 24 hour change percentage. We'll grab the open price, check to see if the price went up or down, and calculate the difference. Using `if` statements we can set + or – symbols before our number and set a color based on whether it went up or down.

{137}
```
$openPrice = $json["open"];
if($openPrice < $lastPrice)
{
        $operator = "+";
        $change = $lastPrice - $openPrice;
        $percent = $change / $openPrice;
        $percent = $percent * 100;
        $percentChange = $operator.number_format($percent, 1);
        $color = "green";
}
if($openPrice > $lastPrice)
{
        $operator = "-";
        $change = $openPrice - $lastPrice;
        $percent = $change / $openPrice;
        $percent = $percent * 100;
        $percentChange = $operator.number_format($percent, 1);
        $color = "red";
}
```

Alright we are almost there. Just the time is left, and then we can start plugging the values in our page. You can do this with PHP using the unix time provided with the API call, but it's much easier by just using the built-in function `date();`

{138}
```
$date = date("m/d/Y - h:i:sa");
```

Here's what you should have in the PHP section now:

{139}
```php
<?php
$url = "https://www.bitstamp.net/api/ticker/";
$fgc = file_get_contents($url);
$json = json_decode($fgc, TRUE);
$lastPrice = $json["last"];
$highPrice = $json["high"];
$lowPrice = $json["low"];
$lastPrice = number_format($lastPrice, 2);
$highPrice = number_format($highPrice, 2);
$lowPrice = number_format($lowPrice, 2);
//calc 24 hr change
$openPrice = $json["open"];
if($openPrice < $lastPrice)
{
        $operator = "+";
        $change = $lastPrice - $openPrice;
        $percent = $change / $openPrice;
        $percent = $percent * 100;
        $percentChange = $operator.number_format($percent, 1);
        $color = "green";
}
if($openPrice > $lastPrice)
{
        $operator = "-";
        $change = $openPrice - $lastPrice;
        $percent = $change / $openPrice;
        $percent = $percent * 100;
        $percentChange = $operator.number_format($percent, 1);
        $color = "red";
}
$date = date("m/d/Y - h:i:sa");

?>
```

7.8 Moving the PHP Values to HTML

Great! Now let's start plugging these values in our page. We'll use `echo` to print out the value of the variables we created. You can jump in and out of HTML, CSS or JavaScript by opening and closing PHP tags.

Our first cell is the last price. Let's insert a $ before our PHP tags since we didn't include it in our PHP, and echo the last price.

{140}
```
<td rowspan="3" width="75%" id="lastPrice">
$<?php echo $lastPrice; ?>
</td>
```

Repeat these similar steps for the remaining values.
Now remember how we set a color for the percentage change? Instead of coloring it in our style tags we will add a property to the <td> with style and color. You will see why we are doing it like this later.

{141}
```
<td align="right" style="color: <?php echo $color; ?>;">
<?php echo $percentChange; ?>%
</td>
```

Double check your code matches up and then give it a spin on your webserver.

{142}
```
<?php
$url = "https://www.bitstamp.net/api/ticker/";
$fgc = file_get_contents($url);
$json = json_decode($fgc, TRUE);
$lastPrice = $json["last"];
$highPrice = $json["high"];
$lowPrice = $json["low"];
$lastPrice = number_format($lastPrice, 2);
$highPrice = number_format($highPrice, 2);
```

```php
$lowPrice = number_format($lowPrice, 2);
//calc 24 hr change
$openPrice = $json["open"];
if($openPrice < $lastPrice)
{
        $operator = "+";
        $change = $lastPrice - $openPrice;
        $percent = $change / $openPrice;
        $percent = $percent * 100;
        $percentChange = $operator.number_format($percent, 1);
        $color = "green";
}
if($openPrice > $lastPrice)
{
        $operator = "-";
        $change = $openPrice - $lastPrice;
        $percent = $change / $openPrice;
        $percent = $percent * 100;
        $percentChange = $operator.number_format($percent, 1);
        $color = "red";
}
$date = date("m/d/Y - h:i:sa");

?>

<!DOCTYPE html>
<html>
<head>
<title>My BTC Widget</title>
<style>
#container{
        width: 275px;
        height: 90px;
        overflow: hidden;
        background-color: #2f2f2f;
        border: 1px solid #000;
        border-radius: 5px;
        color: #fefdfb;
}
#lastPrice{
        font-size: 24px;
        font-weight: bold;
}
#dateTime{
        font-size: 9px;
        color: #999;
}
</style>
</head>
<body>
<div id="container">
<table width="100%">
<tr>
        <td rowspan="3" width="60%" id="lastPrice">
        $<?php echo $lastPrice; ?>
        </td>
```

```
                <td align="right" style="color: <?php echo $color; ?
>;">
                <?php echo $percentChange; ?>%
                </td>
        </tr>
                <td align="right">
                H: <?php echo $highPrice; ?>
                </td>
        <tr>
                <td align="right">
                L: <?php echo $lowPrice; ?>
                </td>
        </tr>
        <tr>
                <td align="right" colspan="2" id="dateTime">
                <?php echo $date; ?>
                </td>
        </tr>
        </table>
        </div>
        </body>
        </html>
```

7.9 Make it Auto Refresh with JavaScript AJAX

If you are looking for simple, you can stop with what you have; the only downside would be that the figures do not auto-refresh live on the page. In order to make it auto-refresh the data on the widget without reloading the entire page we will be using some JavaScript.

AJAX is Asynchronous JavaScript And XML, and is commonly used to refresh parts of a page without having to reload the entire page. We'll be using the asynchronous JavaScript part ;)

The script will use `setTimeout()` to re-run our function every 15 seconds, and the function will be calling data from a PHP source. This will require us to separate our PHP code from our existing HTML and CSS into two files. It will also require several other changes, but let's start with one thing at a time.

Copy the PHP code out of our existing page and save it to a new file, name it data.php. That's everything from `<?php` down to `?>`. We'll get back to the data.php page later.

Back on our existing page, we are going to reference the jQuery library. Insert the jQuery script URL just before the end of the `<head>` tags.

{143}
```
<script src="//code.jquery.com/jquery-1.12.0.min.js">
</script>
```

JQuery works with JavaScript and can make some functions easier to process.

In the body of our HTML after the `<div>` tags close we will insert our JavaScript and jQuery.

Begin by opening our `<script>` tags

```
<script></script>
```

Inside our script tags create a function called `refreshData()`

```
function refreshData(){
};
```

Inside our function we'll use the `load()` built-in function and target our container `<div>`.

```
$('#container').load()
```

Within our `load()` parameters we need to declare what to load, in our case data.php and then separated by a comma we'll create an anonymous function (a function without a name) that will use `setTimeout()` to call our `refreshData()` parent function.

{144}
```
$('#container').load('data.php', function(){
setTimeout(refreshData, 15000);
})
```

So all together we have

{145}
```
<script>
function refreshData(){
    $('#container').load('data.php', function(){
    setTimeout(refreshData, 15000);
    });
}
</script>
```

We have our function that will update our div, to whatever data.php outputs, but we still need to tell it when to run. Prior to the `refreshData` function we created create an anonymous function that calls our `refreshData` function when the document (our page) loads.

{146}
```
<script>
$(document).ready(function(){
refreshData();
});
function refreshData(){
    $('#container').load('data.php', function(){
    setTimeout(refreshData, 15000);
    });
}
</script>
```

Save this and run it.

You should be horrified, as all the data is missing! What happened? Well our jQuery code is telling our page to replace what is inside of our `<div id="container">` with the output of data.php. The output of data.php is nothing. It holds the variables but we need to echo it out for it to display. What this also means is we need to take the HTML code within our container <div> and move it to the php file.

Copy the code from inside the div, from `<table width="100%">` down to `</table>`.

Go to our data.php we created a bit earlier, at at the bottom of our code, create a new variable name it `$table` that equals to all that HTML we just copied. The trick here is we need to wrap it with `<<<EOT EOT;` which is HEREDOC and is intended for large multi-line strings like this.

{147}
```
$table = <<<EOT
<table width="100%">
<tr>
  <td rowspan="3" width="60%" id="lastPrice">
  $<?php echo $lastPrice; ?>
  </td>
  <td align="right" style="color: <?php echo $color; ?>;">
  <?php echo $percentChange; ?>%
  </td>
</tr>
  <td align="right">
  H: <?php echo $highPrice; ?>
  </td>
<tr>
  <td align="right">
  L: <?php echo $lowPrice; ?>
  </td>
</tr>
<tr>
  <td align="right" colspan="2" id="dateTime">
  <?php echo $date; ?>
  </td>
</tr>
</table>
EOT;
```

Okay we are almost done, I promise. Since we are already in PHP tags, we need to remove all of the `<?php ?>` we have in our table and `<td>` tags. We also need to remove the semicolons after our variables since we are using HEREDOC. Then after the `EOT;` echo out the `$table` variable.

{148}
```
$table = <<<EOT
<table width="100%">
<tr>
  <td rowspan="3" width="60%" id="lastPrice">
  $$lastPrice
  </td>
<td align="right" style="color: <?php echo $color; ?>;">
  $percentChange %
  </td>
</tr>
  <td align="right">
  H: $highPrice
  </td>
<tr>
  <td align="right">
  L: $lowPrice
  </td>
</tr>
<tr>
  <td align="right" colspan="2" id="dateTime">
  Powered by: <a href="#" target="_blank">BTCthreads.com</a>
$date
  </td>
</tr>
</table>
EOT;

echo $table;
```

Save everything and run the original file, and if you did everything right you should have a functional widget that refreshes every 15 seconds.

You can make other changes, like add a "Powered by mysite.com" or adjust the font and colors how you'd like.

{149} HTML

```html
<!DOCTYPE html>
<html>
<head>
<title>My BTC Widget</title>
<style>
#container{
      width: 275px;
      height: 90px;
      overflow: hidden;
      background-color: #2f2f2f;
      border: 1px solid #000;
      border-radius: 5px;
      color: #fefdfb;
      font-family: arial;
}
#lastPrice{
      font-size: 34px;
      font-weight: bold;
}
#dateTime{
      font-size: 9px;
      color: #999;
}
#dateTime a{
    color: #ccc;
}
</style>
<script src="//code.jquery.com/jquery-1.12.0.min.js"></script>
</head>
<body>
<div id="container">

</div>
<script>
    $(document).ready(function(){
      refreshData();
    });

    function refreshData(){
        $('#container').load('data.php', function(){
           setTimeout(refreshData, 15000);
        });
    }
</script>
</body>
</html>
```

{150}PHP

```php
<?php
$url = "https://www.bitstamp.net/api/ticker/";
$fgc = file_get_contents($url);
$json = json_decode($fgc, TRUE);
$lastPrice = $json["last"];
$highPrice = $json["high"];
$lowPrice = $json["low"];
$lastPrice = number_format($lastPrice, 2);
$highPrice = number_format($highPrice, 2);
$lowPrice = number_format($lowPrice, 2);
//calc 24 hr change
$openPrice = $json["open"];
if($openPrice < $lastPrice)
{
	$operator = "+";
	$change = $lastPrice - $openPrice;
	$percent = $change / $openPrice;
	$percent = $percent * 100;
	$percentChange = $operator.number_format($percent, 1);
	$color = "green";
}
if($openPrice > $lastPrice)
{
	$operator = "-";
	$change = $openPrice - $lastPrice;
	$percent = $change / $openPrice;
	$percent = $percent * 100;
	$percentChange = $operator.number_format($percent, 1);
	$color = "red";
}
$date = date("m/d/Y - h:i:sa");

$table = <<<EOT
<table width="100%">
<tr>
	<td rowspan="3" width="60%" id="lastPrice">
	$$lastPrice
	</td>
	<td align="right" id="percentChange" style="color: $color;">
	 $percentChange %
	</td>
</tr>
	<td align="right">
	H: $highPrice
	</td>
<tr>
	<td align="right">
	L: $lowPrice
	</td>
</tr>
<tr>
	<td align="right" colspan="2" id="dateTime">
```

```
        Powered by: <a href="#"
target="_blank">BTCthreads.com</a> $date
        </td>
</tr>
</table>
EOT;

echo $table;

?>
```

PRO TIP: You can avoid hitting API request limits by using an exchange's websocket instead. A websocket will also automatically refresh the page, eliminating a lot of additional work. Bitfinex for example has a free websocket at `wss://api2.bitfinex.com:3000/ws`. The websocket stream provides the latest price, the high, low, daily percentage change, and more. Everything you need to make a widget.

Find out more about Bitfinex's websocket at http://docs.bitfinex.com

Below is a simple example of getting the latest price with Bitfinex's websocket.

{150bfx}
```
<html>
<div id="btc"></div>
<script>
var ws = new WebSocket("wss://api2.bitfinex.com:3000/ws");
ws.onopen = function(){
  ws.send(JSON.stringify({"event":"subscribe", "channel":"ticker", "pair":"BTCUSD"}))
};
ws.onmessage = function(msg){
  var response = JSON.parse(msg.data);
  var hb = response[1];
  if(hb != "hb"){
    document.getElementById("btc").innerHTML = "$" + response[7];
  }
};
</script>
</html>
```

8. Third Party APIs

Third party APIs offer developers a way to work with the Bitcoin network without having to run a full Bitcoin node. Running a full node could be too expensive, or have requirements that they cannot meet. Renting a VPS that can support the bandwidth and storage space for a full node could be quite costly for the average hobbyist developer. This is where APIs come into play.

8.1 Which API to Use?

There are several options available for developers when choosing a third party API. My personal favorite is Blockchain.info.

Here are some popular and trusted API services:

Blockchain.info – Free API service for merchants and developers. You must request an API key prior to using the wallet APIs. They also have a public API on blockchain statistics that does not require an API key.

BitPay – One of the most popular for merchants to accept bitcoin. Requires an application process prior to usage.

Coinbase – API for merchants is available, a review and application process is required.

Blocktrail – Free API services for developers.

Block.io – Free for basic and limited usage. Requires subscription to use certain features, or after reaching a certain number of used addresses.

Blockcypher – Free API services for developers.

Various Exchanges – Nearly every exchange has public APIs to query statistics. Some exchanges have private APIs you can sign up for to make trades using their API.

When building bitcoin sites it is okay to use more than one API service at a time or even mix using JSON-RPC with a bitcoin node and third party APIs. Use whatever you need to, to get the job done.

8.2 Working with JSON

When using third party APIs the vast majority will send your web server responses in JavaScript Object Notation (JSON). JSON format is easily interpreted by most programming languages, which is why it is widely used with APIs.

It may seem a bit confusing at first, but after spending a little time with JSON you should pick it up pretty quickly.

Reading JSON basically has two parts, being able to identify objects and identify keys. Here's an example of a key:

```
"last": 407.26
```

Here's an example of an object:

```
"person":{ "name": "Kyle", "age": 31}
```

In this example person is an object, and within the object holds two keys.

When working with JSON objects you must access the objects first prior to accessing the keys. For example let's say we have a key of "name" but it is nested inside an object called "person". In order to access the name you would call `["person"]["name"]`.

What if you had a multiple arrays inside of an object, like this:

```
"employees":[
    {
        "name":"John",
        "age":32
    },
    {
```

```
        "name":"Sam",
        "age":26
    }
]
```

Now if you tried `["employees"]["name"]`, your script would fail because the program doesn't know which entry you are referring to. You need to add in the increment to clarify which entry you are referring to. To get John's age you would access it like `["employees"][0]["age"]`. Zero refers to the first array, so to get Sam's age you would do `["employees"][1]["age"]`.

So if any of your JSON request are failing take a look and see if there is a bracket [in your key.

```
        "key":[
```

This indicates an array, and you will need to specify the increment when calling keys within.

This is crucial to understand because when working with third party APIs and bitcoind, the built-in bitcoin API for bitcoin nodes, you will be doing this a lot.

For example this is what part of a transaction looks like in bitcoind:

```
{
    "amount" : 0.00120000,
    "confirmations" : 3535,
    "blockhash" : "00000000000000000a50ce874471a2fa70629639ec11f20e1ef4077d9b673cb5",
    "blockindex" : 124,
    "blocktime" : 1449452004,
    "txid" : "6ad94d98cc4af42f2e2d09aa13940e97d4bc8d24418ccd246c508332479a16f7",
    "walletconflicts" : [
    ],
```

```
    "time" : 1449451975,
    "timereceived" : 1449451975,
    "details" : [
        {
            "account" : "raw",
            "address" : "15PgcEkCBv93aNJfJGtCWxPDtLetbCkPxV",
            "category" : "receive",
            "amount" : 0.00120000,
            "vout" : 0
        }
    ],
    "hex" : "0100000001a9ee419a5ae13eb2ed7638a061e6c577410ec6273c96e2a2ffaaef400ed6844c010000006b483045022100afb90814e17d5d51a70c37069c9328da0baaf700c56f4ec47f6c008e72468efd0220421eb348290695a54b428f1f986042121b5ab25f4c81727dba0f6a2bf1d56ae30121024c74bc61423f42f394fdd044da0233a1f1b68aa2f6d3b5c7cec25eb83c8af81ffffffff02c0d40100000000001976a914302ab78d3da3580bdbd7a15253454fe35dd14ff288acf07e0e00000000001976a914bc20526aca4c47b805511abc6b81d4f15dc3f38c88ac00000000"
}
```

8.3 Blockchain.info API

Blockchain.info has public API for statistics on the blockchain as well a free merchant API system. The two main merchant API services they offer are the Receive Payments and a full Wallet API.

The Receive Payments API is only for receiving payments. The full Wallet API allows receiving and sending of funds.

8.4 Receive Payments API

Blockchain.info rolled out their new receive payments API on November 23, 2015. This will be replacing the previous version of the receive payments API. Any requests using the old version will fail. The new version uses Hierarchical Deterministic (HD) keys, but other than that both versions are pretty similar. In this section I will show you the differences and how to use the new HD BIP32 xpub receive payments API.

The main difference with the new version is that it uses deterministic addresses, specifically BIP32. This uses an extended public key (xpub) to generate all future addresses in a deterministic way. This ensures that you can generate the exact same addresses in the future as long as you still have your extended public and private keys. Using this technology blockchain.info was able to drop the forwarding of funds that they used in the previous version. All the addresses generated will already be owned under the extended private key. The callback feature still works the same as it did in the previous version, which allows notifications to be sent to your webserver once a payment has been received.

Here's what you'll need to start using the new version of the receive payments API.

- API Key (https://api.blockchain.info/v2/apikey/request/)
- BIP32 xpub key

That's it! The BIP32 extended public key can be one from an outside wallet like Multibit or you can use blockchain.info's new HD wallet.

8.5 Initiate the Request Using cURL

Start a new file and open up your PHP tags. The first thing we are going to do is create a new variable and call it `$api_key`.

```
<?php
$api_key = "your_api_key";
?>
```

Next you will need an extended public key variable. You can use your own from an outside wallet or you can use one from blockchain.info.

```
$xpub = "your_xpub";
```

Then we are going to create another variable to give this a little bit of security. It is a secret code that you make up and it is there to prevent malicious users from trying to manually execute your callback URL.

```
$secret = "really_strong_password";
```

Then we will specify our root URL of where we will be executing this code.

```
$rootURL = "http://yourwebsite.com";
```

Now we are going to create an order ID variable. This will be a unique ID that is unique for every new user that comes to your site. This way you can track orders and know which payments pertain to which orders.

```
$orderID = uniqid();
```

PRO TIP: `uniqid()` is a built in PHP function that creates unique identifiers. It works off of micro-seconds so the odds of two ever being the same is astronomically small.

Create another variable and it will be to identify our callback URL location. We haven't created this page yet. So whatever you name this, you will need to make sure you name your callback the same in the next section.

```
$callback_url = $rootURL."/callback.php";
```

Then we can add in some custom parameters. One is the orderID that we created, we can add that in by using a GET, which is basically stuffing it into the URL.

```
$callback_url = $rootURL."/callback.php?invoice=".$orderID;
```

Then we can also add our secret variable the same way.

```
$callback_url = $rootURL."/callback.php?invoice=".$orderID."&secret=".$secret;
```

Now that we have all the preliminary information. We can make a call to blockchain.info to initiate the call via cURL.

First we'll enter in the blockchain receive payment API endpoint, and include our API key, xPUB and callback.

{151}
```
$receive_url = "https://api.blockchain.info/v2/receive?key=".
$api_key."&xpub=".$xpub."&callback=.".url_encode($callback);
```

Now we will create a cURL request.

Initiate and execute, you can think of these like open and close PHP tags.

```
$ch = curl_init();
$ccc = curl_exec($ch);
```

Now we can set our cURL options in between the initiate and execution.

Verify the SSL certificate since blockchain uses HTTPS:
```
curl_setopt($ch, CURLOPT_SSL_VERIFYPEER, true);
```

Return the contents as a string:
```
curl_setopt($ch, CURLOPT_RETURNTRANSFER, true);
```

Tell cURL where to go:
```
curl_setopt($ch, CURLOPT_URL, $receive_url);
```

Together it will look like:

{152}
```
$ch = curl_init();
curl_setopt($ch, CURLOPT_SSL_VERIFYPEER, true);
curl_setopt($ch, CURLOPT_RETURNTRANSFER, true);
curl_setopt($ch, CURLOPT_URL, $receive_url);
$ccc = curl_exec($ch);
```

When blockchain responds it will be in JSON format, so we'll need to decode it.

```
$json = json_decode($ccc, true);
```

The address that blockchain creates based on the xpub will be returned under "address"

```
$payTo = json["address"];
```

Then we can just echo it out

```
echo $payTo
```

index.php
{153}
```
$api_key = "your_blockchain_api_Key";
$xpub = "xpubYour_extended_public_key";
$secret = "your_secret"; //this can be anything you want
$rootURL = "http://yourrooturl.com/directory";
$orderID = uniqid();

$callback_url = $rootURL."/callback.php?invoice=".
$orderID."&secret=".$secret;
$receive_url = "https://api.blockchain.info/v2/receive?key=".
$api_key."&xpub=".
$xpub."&callback=".urlencode($callback_url);
$ch = curl_init();
curl_setopt($ch, CURLOPT_SSL_VERIFYPEER, true);
curl_setopt($ch, CURLOPT_RETURNTRANSFER, true);
curl_setopt($ch, CURLOPT_URL, $receive_url);
$ccc = curl_exec($ch);
$json = json_decode($ccc, true);
$payTo = $json['address'];

echo $payTo;
```

Save the above as a PHP file, and run it on your server. If you did everything correctly you should see a fresh address on the screen. The callback can include any custom information you would like, in this example I only included an order/invoice number and a secret.

8.6 Implementing the Callback

Now let's get into creating the callback page. Start a new file, and open and close your PHP tags. First we'll begin by verifying our secret variable.

{154}
```
$secret = "your_secret";
if($_GET['secret'] != $secret){
die('stop doing that');
}
```

We grabbed the secret from the URL using a GET and then we compared the two.

We should also include an `else`, or tell the file what to do if the secrets do match. If the secrets do match then that means we received a payment.

At this point it's really up to you what you want it to do, the most important part though is that you echo out `*ok*`, make sure it is between *'s.

```
else {
echo "*ok*";
}
```

This will tell blockchain.info that you received their notification. If you do not do this they will continue to send you notifications and thus your callback page will run 1,000 times for the next 1,000 blocks.

callback.php
{155}
```
$secret = "your_secret";
   if($_GET['secret'] != $secret)
   {
```

```
      die('Stop doing that');
    }
    else
    {
$order_num = $_GET['invoice'];
$amount = $_GET['value'];
$amountCalc = $amount / 100000000; //optional

$queryUpdate = "UPDATE orders SET paid = 1, recd = $amount
WHERE orderid = '$order_num'";

$doUpdate = mysqli_query($conn, $queryUpdate) or
die(mysqli_error($conn));
    if($doUpdate)
        {
        echo "*ok*";
        }
    }
```

Using `$_GET`s we can get information about the transaction. The following GETs are automatically provided on every request.

- `$_GET['value']` - How much bitcoin was received, in satoshis
- `$_GET['confirmations']` - The number of confirmations for this transaction
- `$_GET['address']` - The address that was generated to receive the payment
- `$_GET['transaction_hash']` - The transaction hash for this transaction

For additional security against double spends you could use the confirmation parameter to only update your database once you have a certain number of confirmations.

Using the blockchain receive payments API is great for merchants who want to be able to accept bitcoin online. You could also use it to start an online fundraiser for a group or charity. You could use it to create a pay-per-post system, or a paywall to monetize web content. The different possible uses is nearly endless. It's completely free and requires no credit checks like most shopping cart payments processors do.

8.7 Blockchain Wallet API

As of January 2016, Blockchain.info made changes to the wallet API service that now requires you to run a local nodeJS service to handle the calls. This will require root access to the webserver so you will need to use a VPS instead of a basic shared web host.

In my examples I will be using DigitalOcean to run a $5/month VPS. Some users have reported that their VPS crashes a lot on the $5/month plan, so if you are building for production you should consider using a more powerful/expensive plan.

8.8 Wallet API Setup

If you haven't already, create a wallet with blockchain.info. During the process make sure you register and validate your email address.

Once created you will need an API key for their Wallet API.
https://blockchain.info/api/api_create_code
This API key is different than the Receive Payments API key.

Allow API access, in your wallet settings. You can do this by logging in to your blockchain wallet, go to account settings, then IP Restrictions and then check the box to allow API access.

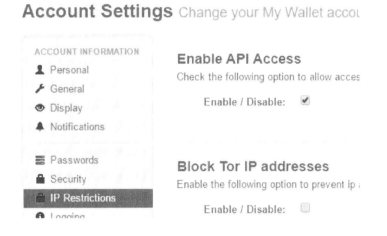

8.9 VPS Setup

Once registered with Digital Ocean, create a new droplet.

When prompted to choose an OS, switch to the One-Click-Apps tab and choose the MEAN stack.

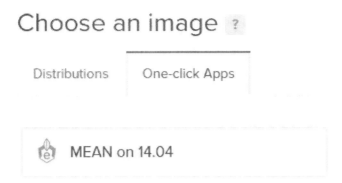

You can leave the other options at their default settings and click CREATE. DigitalOcean will now create a new VPS with the MEAN stack pre-configured.

You will receive an email with your password and server details.

Go to your droplets section on DigitalOcean and access the console.

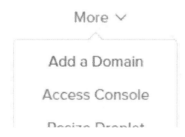

Type in root and hit ENTER

Enter the password, and you will be prompted to create a new password.

TIP: At this point it's a good idea to create a user instead of using root. See the next chapter, Section 9.1.

Now you are in and it's time to install NodeJS. The next part type what you see and hit enter after each one.

```
sudo apt-get update

sudo apt-get install nodejs
```

Press Y to accept

```
sudo apt-get install npm
```

Press Y to accept

```
npm install -g blockchain-wallet-service
```

Now the blockchain wallet service is being installed onto your VPS. It's normal if you see some warnings or errors during the install process.

Once installed, navigate to the installed folder and check the version to see if it installed properly.

```
cd ..
cd usr/local/bin
node blockchain-wallet-service -V
```

If it installed correctly, you should see a version number.

The wallet service is now installed and you can use it with NodeJS. But what if you wanted to use PHP instead? For that we will need to install apache and PHP.

```
sudo apt-get update

sudo apt-get install apache2

sudo apt-get install php5 libapache2-mod-php5

sudo apt-get install php5-mcrypt

sudo apt-get install php5-curl

reboot
```

Your VPS is now restarting after all the changes. Once restarted navigate back to usr/local/bin.

```
cd usr/local/bin
```

Now we can launch our wallet:

```
node blockchain-wallet-service start -port 3030
```

It should respond with confirmation that it is running.

8.10 Initiate Login

Now that it is running, before we can make calls, we have to login to verify our credentials with blockchain.info.

We do that by sending a request to our nodeJS service at:

```
http://127.0.0.1:3030/merchant/YOUR-GUID/login?password=YOUR-PASSWORD&api_code=YOUR_API_KEY
```

You can do this with a `file_get_contents()` or cURL.

Login example using cURL

login.php

{156}
```
$url = "http://127.0.0.1:3030/merchant/YOUR-GUID/login?password=YOUR-PASSWORD&api_code=YOUR-API-CODE";
$ch = curl_init();
curl_setopt($ch, CURLOPT_SSL_VERIFYPEER, false);
curl_setopt($ch, CURLOPT_RETURNTRANSFER, true);
curl_setopt($ch, CURLOPT_URL, $url);
$ccc = curl_exec($ch);
$json = json_decode($ccc, true);
echo "<pre>";
var_dump($json);
echo "</pre>";
```

Save the above and run it on your server. The file should keep spinning and loading since blockchain.info doesn't recognize the IP address. Wait for it to timeout, about 60 seconds, and then check your email. Blockchain should have sent you an API access attempt showing what IP tried to connect. Follow the link and authorize the attempt, also take your servers IP address from the email and whitelist it in your account settings. (Login->Account Settings->IP Restrictions).

Now try running the PHP file again.

If you did everything correctly you should see a response that lists your GUID followed by `Success TRUE`.

You're now connected and you can start sending requests with your wallet.

8.11 Creating Addresses

To create a fresh address we can use the cURL example from the above login and just change the `$url` variable.

{157}
```
$url = "http://127.0.0.1:3030/merchant/YOUR-
GUID/new_address?password=YOUR-PASSWORD&api_code=YOUR-
API-CODE";
```

Notice the only thing we changed was after YOUR-GUID, from `/login` to `/new_address`. If you run this, it will return with a new address in JSON.

Example response:
```
{"address": "1NPrfWgJfkANmd1jt88A141PjhiarT8d9U"}
```

You can also include a label, to tie addresses to specific orders or users.

{158}
```
/new_address?password=YOUR-PASSWORD&api_code=YOUR-API-
CODE&label=ORDER_ID";
```

Example response:
```
{"address": "1NPrfWgJfkANmd1jt88A141PjhiarT8d9U",
 "label":"ORDER_ID"}
```

8.12 Sending Funds

Now that we can receive funds, we might also want to send funds to users. In the same manner that we logged in, and created a new address, we can send funds just by changing that `$url` variable.

{159}
```
/payment?password=PW&api_code=YOUR-API-CODE&to=BTC_ADDY&amount=20000";
```

Notice we only changed `/new_address` to `/payment`, and then we added two required parameters `to` and `amount`. `To` is what address will receive the payment and `amount` is the amount in satoshis. It takes 100,000,000 satoshis to make 1 whole bitcoin, so keep that in mind when specifying amounts.

A successful payment will respond with details of the transaction and a transaction ID in JSON format:

```
{
  "to" : ["1NPrfWgJfkANmd1jt88A141PjhiarT8d9U"],
  "from": ["1J9ikqFuwrzPbczsDkquA9uVYeq6dEehsj"],
  "amounts": [200000],
  "fee": 1000,
  "txid": "4653a9c72e38d9474cf22b5ba1cbea3e7bbdf06a734936cdc462799357fa8299",
  "success": true
}
```

Notice that the fields: to, from and amounts are arrays as there can be multiple values.

Some other popular calls are getting balance of your entire wallet:

{160}
```
/balance?password=PW&api_code=YOUR-API-CODE
```

Getting balance of a specific address:

{161}
```
/address_balance?password=PW&api_code=YOUR-API-CODE&address=SOME_ADDRESS
```

You can find a full list of calls and examples at blockchain.info's API documentation page.
 https://github.com/blockchain/service-my-wallet-v3

9. Bitcoind JSON-RPC API

We have already went over some third party APIs, but we have not touched the API that is built-in with Bitcoin. There are two types of the Bitcoin software: the visually friendly UI version and the command daemon version.

Using the API is not very difficult; the part that I think most people have trouble with is the setup.

You need to decide if you want to host your node on a VPS, or at home with a PC that will be on and connected to the internet 24/7. The latter choice is less common and not possible for everyone. The problem that comes with hosting on a VPS is the cost for a service that can handle the requirements of the Bitcoin client software.

Both options have their perks, and you need to choose which one is right for your needs. If you are just developing as a hobby and you don't plan on launching a live service, I would recommend that you try to host one at home. If you plan on running a live service that will be the back-bone to your website, I suggest you run with a dedicated VPS.

9.1 Setup

In order to use the API we need to run a full node Bitcoin client in server mode.

If you haven't already done so, download the latest Bitcoin client software.

If using at home PC: Search for the latest Bitcoin client release and download. At the time of writing, the latest release is available at bitcoin.org. Follow the install instructions. Skip to section 9.2 Config and Options.

If using a Linux VPS: Login to your VPS command line via SSH (Easy Way: DigitalOcean VPS has a built-in console window).

Create a new droplet, select one-click apps and choose the LAMP stack. This will install Apache, PHP and MySQL for us upfront so we won't have to on the command-line.

Access your VPS using the Console Access feature. You should see a blank black screen. Click on the screen, type in "root" and hit enter.
```
root
```

Now it will prompt you for your password. The password to access was emailed you right after you created the droplet, so check your email for the password. Enter in your password and it will prompt you to create a new one.

Great now we're in. Before we start firing off more commands, let's create a new user. Operating under root is not advised and can possibly be destructive since root has so many privileges.

Create a new user:
```
adduser satoshi
```

It will then prompt you to create a password for your new user. It will also ask for additional information that is not required so you can skip those by just pressing ENTER.

Now let's grant our new user some additional privileges by making them a super-user.
```
gpasswd -a satoshi sudo
```

Logout of the root account using the logout command:
```
logout
```

You can now login as your new user.

Great now we can install bitcoind by using the following commands.

Update your packages
```
sudo apt-get update
```

Get bitcoin package
```
sudo apt-add-repository ppa:bitcoin/bitcoin
```

Update again
```
sudo apt-get update
```

Install
```
sudo apt-get install bitcoind -y
```

Reboot
```
sudo reboot
```

After rebooting confirm bitcoin was installed by calling and running bitcoind.
```
bitcoind
```

Give it a few minutes to start running, and then you can kill the program with ctrl+Z. Verify that bitcoind started and created the necessary local files. Navigate to the hidden folder in your root directory. Type in
```
cd ~/.bitcoin
```

If it changed directories, then Bitcoin was installed. You can confirm with print working directory.
```
pwd
```

Or you see the files and directories that were created by typing ls.
```
ls
```

9.2 Config and Options

Now that Bitcoin is installed we need to configure it. We do this by creating a bitcoin.conf file and setting our options inside of it.

Create a new file in your text editor

{162}
```
rpcuser=someusername
rpcpassword=somepassword
daemon=1
keypool=10000
prune=600
maxuploadtarget=20
maxconnections=16
```

Now save the file as bitcoin.conf in your /bitcoin directory. On a Linux VPS you may need to do sudo apt-get update first. Bitcoin will be installed in ~/.bitcoin

If you are using a VPS, you can sftp using an FTP program such as Filezilla. Your login credentials will be the same as when you SSH to your VPS: IP address, root or username, and password. Locate your bitcoin directory and save your conf file there.

Something that is special about this conf file versus other examples you will find online is we are intentionally limiting the resources this node will use. `Prune` will make it so that we don't store the entire blockchain to save disk space. `Maxuploadtarget` and `maxconnections` will limit data transmitted to peers to save on bandwidth. Some people might see this as controversial because we are running a selfish node that will allow us to transact with other nodes, but give back very little to the network in order to save on resources.

Running a full node without restrictions will use over 60GB of hard drive space as of time of this writing, and this continues to grow every day. If you don't cap bandwidth you will be using over 600 GB of bandwidth per month. A VPS that can handle these numbers can be very expensive, which is why we are taking the selfish node approach.

9.3 Run and Test

Now you can execute bitcoind and let it sync with the network. If you are using a VPS just navigate to your bitcoin directory and type in bitcoind.

```
bitcoind
```

You can verify the status of your node by typing

```
bitcoin-cli getinfo
```

Now we wait for Bitcoin to validate all the blocks and transactions. Even though it is a pruned node it is still a fully validating node.

The initial bandwidth used to download the full blockchain will be much greater than after it has synced.

9.4 Your First JSON-RPC Calls

Now that all blocks have been validated and your bitcoind is fully synced you are ready to start making calls. We will be using PHP to communicate with our node. If you check the bitcoin wiki JSON-RPC page you will see references for many different languages.

The library recommended for PHP is the EasyBitcoin-PHPLibarary.

The easiest way to get the library is to visit the GitHub page, https://github.com/aceat64/EasyBitcoin-PHP.

Click on the easybitcoin.php file in the GitHub repository.

The easybitcoin library makes cURL requests to bitcoind's JSON-RPC 8332 port.

Copy the contents of the easybitcoin.php and save it as a new php file called easybitcoin.php. Make sure you place this file in your web server directory as you will need to `require();` it in you PHP code.

Create a new file and start with your PHP tags.

```
<?php ?>
```

First require the easybitcoin library file.

{163}
```
require("easybitcoin.php");
```

Then create a new variable called `$bitcoin` and use the `Bitcoin()` function to authenticate with your node using your RPC username and password that you created in the bitcoin.conf file.

{164}
```
$bitcoin = new Bitcoin("username", "somepassword");
```

Great, now we can make an RPC call. Let's do `getinfo` as our first call.

```
$info = $bitcoin->getinfo();
```

This will grab info on our node, and return it in JSON format. So let's dump it so we can see everything that comes back.

```
print_r($info);
```

All together you should have:

{165}
```
<?php
require("easybitcoin.php");
$bitcoin = new Bitcoin("username", "somepassword");
$info = $bitcoin->getinfo();
print_r($info);
?>
```

Save this as a PHP file, upload it to your server. You should see an output that looks like this:

```
Array([version]=>120000 [protocolversion]=> 70012
[walletversion]=> 60000 [balance]=> 0.012
[blocks]=> 406108 ...
```

This is an array print out of the `getinfo` command.

We can change `getinfo();` to `getbalance();` and instead all it will print out is the balance.

```
$info = $bitcoin->getbalance();
```

If you make that small change and save and run it you should see something like:

```
0.012
```

9.5 Creating Addresses

You can also create new addresses, by changing `getbalance()` to `getnewaddress();`. If you want to add a label for this new address just include it in the parenthesis.

{166}
```
$info = $bitcoin->getnewaddress("Nakamoto");
```

You will see a brand new bitcoin address that has been added to your node and can start accepting transactions.

Pretty neat! If you now change `getnewaddress();` to `listaccounts();` it will print out all the different labels and their balance.

{167}
```
$info = $bitcoin->listaccounts();
```

Let's briefly talk about implementation. You can make it so that all new users that sign up on your site will be given a new address to make payments to. Now you can either just add a unique user ID as the label like:

{168}
```
$uid = uniqid();
$info = $bitcoin->getnewaddress($uid);
```

Or store that address and their user ID to a database.

{169}
```
$uid = uniqid();
$info = $bitcoin->getnewaddress();
$add = $db->prepare("INSERT INTO users (userid, address) VALUES (?, ?)");
```

Using labels is NOT RECOMMENDED, because it does not scale well beyond a few thousand accounts. A database like MySQL would perform better and allow you to have millions of users without causing any slowness.

9.6 Sending Payments

The circle wouldn't be complete if we could only receive payments, but not send them. The easiest way to send bitcoin is by using `sendtoaddress();`.

{170}
```
$send = $bitcoin->sendtoaddress("1SomeBitcoinAddy", 1);
```

The first argument for `sendtoaddress()` is the address you want to send funds to, the second is the amount in whole bitcoins. So the above would send a whole bitcoin to 1SomeBitcoinAddy.

If this is a success your bitcoin node will respond with the transaction ID. But what if there was an error? Errors will be stored in `$bitcoin->error`. Below is an example of a ternary operator to handle an error.

{171}
```
$send = $bitcoin->sendtoaddress("1SomeBitcoinAddy", 1);
echo $send ? $send : "Oops an error: ".$bitcoin->error;
```

If there is an error the page will print "Oops an error : <some reason>", if it is a success the page will print the transaction ID.

You can also send from specific accounts if you are using labels, again not recommended due to scaling.

{172}
```
$send = $bitcoin->sendfrom("fromLabel","1someBTCAddy" 0.5);
```

9.7 List of Commands

Below are some of the most common commands you will use when using JSON-RPC.

```
getaccount("1someAddress");
```
Gets the account name associated with the address.

```
getaccountaddress("AccountName");
```
Gets the receiving address associated with the account name. If account name does not already exist, a new one will be created along with a new address.

```
getaddressesbyaccount("AccountName");
```
Lists all the addresses associated with the account name.

```
getbalance("AccountName", 2);
```
Returns the current balance for the account name with funds that have at least 2 confirmations.

```
getbalance();
```
Returns the current balance for the ENTIRE bitcoind server.

```
getblockcount();
```
Fetches current block height.

```
getblockhash(420000);
```
Returns the block hash of the specified block height.

```
getblockcount("00000000someHash");
```
Gets block data on the specified block hash.

```
getinfo();
```
Returns data on your node and general data on the blockchain.

```
getnewaddress();
```
Creates a new address with no account name.

```
getnewaddress("SomeAccount");
```
Creates a new address with an account name.

```
getrawmempool();
```
Returns all transaction IDs currently in your mempool.

```
getrawtransaction("64b15someTXID", 1);
```
Returns decoded transaction data in JSON format.

```
gettransaction("64b1SomeTXID");
```
Returns a data object on specified transaction ID.

```
listaccounts();
```
Returns all account names and their corresponding balances.

```
getreceivedbyaccount("AccountName", 1);
```
Returns total amount received by account with at least 1 confirmation.

```
getreceivedbyaddress("1someAddress", 1);
```
Returns total amount received by address with at least 1 confirmation. Does not work on addresses that are not in your wallet.

```
sendtoaddress("1SomeAddress", 0.25);
```
Sends 0.25 BTC to 1SomeAddress

Find the full list of JSON RPC calls for bitcoin at the bitcoin wiki page:
https://en.bitcoin.it/wiki/Original_Bitcoin_client/API_calls_list

PRO TIP: If you are looking for examples of responses or outputs from using these commands, check out the bitcoin developer's reference: https://bitcoin.org/en/developer-reference

10. Databases

A key part of creating interactive and dynamic websites is the use of databases. In simple terms databases are like excel spreadsheets that hold data. Databases can be used to store usernames, passwords, chart data, blog posts, and entire articles. In the Bitcoin world a lot of sites are specific to each user, and in order to create these types of sites you need to use a database. For example, Bob creates an account on your site, signs in, deposits bitcoin, and has his own personal balance. Features such as these are done through the use of a database.

There is more than just one type of database, the most popular however is MySQL, you may have heard of it before. In this book we will using MySQL since this book concentrates on the LAMP stack. I should be able to address the widest audience this way because MySQL typically comes pre-installed on many hosting plans.

10.1 Creating the Database

Start by logging into your cPanel with your webhost. Most hosting providers provide cPanel with their hosting including GoDaddy, HostGator, NameCheap, and more. If you aren't sure if your host has cPanel go to yourdomain.com/cpanel if a login screen appears, then you have cPanel.

After logging in navigate to the database area, and look for MySQL Database Wizard.

The wizard is a quick way to setup a database. It will guide you through creating the database, users, passwords, and privileges. You can also create the databases and users manually, but I suggest using the wizard when creating your first few databases.

Enter a name for your new database in the New Database input box.

Create a username and password that will be allowed to make changes and manipulate the database.

IT'S IMPORTANT TO SAVE THE NAME OF YOUR DATABASE, USERNAME, AND PASSWORD AS YOU WILL NEED IT LATER.

Select the privileges that you want to grant the user. I suggest granting all privileges until you gain more experience in working with databases. It's riskier security-wise but makes things much easier when starting out.

10.2 Creating a Database Table

Return to your cPanel home page. In the same area where you found the MySQL Database Wizard you should also see a PHPMyAdmin icon.

PHPMyAdmin is a popular UI for managing databases without having to compose your own SQL code.

Creating a new table in PHP & SQL code looks something like this:

```
// Create new table called donate
$sql = "CREATE TABLE donate (
postn INT(6) UNSIGNED AUTO_INCREMENT PRIMARY KEY,
postid VARCHAR(50) NOT NULL,
paid VARCHAR(1) DEFAULT'N' NOT NULL,
amount INT(30),
donor VARCHAR(20) NOT NULL,
note VARCHAR(150)
)";
```

Kind of complicated, isn't it? PHPMyAdmin makes it so you can just fill out a form, and click a button to create tables.

If you haven't already, open PHPMyAdmin.

On the left-hand side you should see the new database you just created with the wizard. Make sure it is selected by clicking on it. Now let's create a table within our database.

Under the section labeled "Create Table" we will enter the name of our table, and the number of columns. Then click "Go".

Example:
```
Name:    siteusers
Number of columns: 3
```

Now you will be prompted to a new screen to specify the structure of the table, and what type of content each column can accept.

In this example we have three columns for a table that keeps track of users on our site. Now we need to setup each column.

The first column will be 'userid', this will be a unique id we give to each new user so that we can easily identify them. We will also mark this column as our primary key which will put a constraint on this field that requires it to be a unique value and not empty. This way if somehow our website code fails and creates a duplicate or blank user id the entry will be rejected by the database causing an error.

Additionally, we need to specify the length, and type of content for this column. For userid we'll put a length of 15 characters, and select VARCHAR for type so it can accept various characters including numbers, letters, and symbols.

Field: userid
Type: VARCHAR
Length: 15
Attributes: Primary Key

The second column will be 'username'. Make its type VARCHAR and length 20.

Field: username
Type: VARCHAR
Length: 20

Lastly, we will make our third column address. Make its type VARCHAR and length 40, the longest bitcoin addresses should only be 35 characters long.

Field: address
Type: VARCHAR
Length: 40

Then click "Save".

Congratulations! Your first database is now set up and ready to use!

10.3 Connecting to your Database with PHP

Now that we have a database to work with let's move back over to our editor, and write some PHP to interact with our database.

We will be using the MySQLi PHP extension which should be pre-installed with most servers.

Create a new file, insert your PHP tags, and we're going to connect to our database using `mysqli_connect()`. `Mysqli_connect()` requires 4 inputs, the host, username, password, and database name in that order.

```
$conn = mysqli_connect("localhost","user","pw","siteusers");
```

Make sure you change "user" and "pw" to your actual username and password. If you didn't use "siteusers" as your database name make sure you change that as well.

Now the variable `$db` holds the database credentials that will allow us to connect. Anytime we make a change or request data from our database we will need to use the `$db` variable.

Let's test to see if our connection is working by checking for connection errors.

```
if(mysqli_connect_errno()){
die("Connection to DB failed" .
mysqli_connect_error($conn));
}
```

In the above code we are checking to see if any errors are reporting. If so then we will kill the script and output the error reason to the screen.

We can now save this file, and check to see if our connection works.

database.php

{173}
```php
<?php
$conn = mysqli_connect("localhost","user","pw","siteusers");

if(mysqli_connect_errno()){
die("Connection to DB failed" .
mysqli_connect_error($conn));
}
?>
```

Save it as a PHP file, and upload it to your server. If you see an empty blank page, then your connection was a success. If there was an error, it will be printed on the screen. You should be able to resolve the error easily based on the error message.

10.4 Inserting Data

A database is pretty useless without any data in it, so let's add an entry to our "siteusers" table we created.

Remember our table has three columns: userid, username, and address; we will need to create a variable to define each one before we insert it into our table.

{174}
```php
$uid = uniqid();
$username = "coinableS";
$addy = "1NPrfWgJfkANmd1jt88A141PjhiarT8d9U";
```

The `uniqid()` is a built-in PHP function that creates a unique alpha-numeric string. The strings are unique because they are created based on micro-seconds. The chances of a collision on a single system should be nearly impossible.

We will then create a variable with SQL to insert the data to our table.

{175}
```
$addUser = "INSERT INTO siteusers (userid, username,
address) VALUES('$uid', '$username', '$addy')");
```

Inside our SQL command we begin by telling it that we want to add some data to the table by declaring INSERT INTO. Afterwards we specify which table we want to add data to, in this case "siteusers". Then we specify which columns in the table we are adding our data (userid, username, address). The last part, VALUES is what data we want to add to the columns in their respective order.

Respective order matters! If instead you wrote ($username, $uid, $addy); your database will be populated with the username in the userid field, and the userid data in the username field! Pay attention to what order you enter your columns in relationship to the order of your values.

Now we need to execute this command to our database. We're going to create a new variable and use `mysqli_query` to execute the SQL.

{176}
```
$doAddUser = mysqli_query($conn, $addUser) or
die(mysqli_error($conn));
```

The first parameter in `mysqli()` is our connection variable `$conn`, and the second is the SQL command that we want to execute.

The second-half will kill the script, and output an error reason if there is an error inserting the data to the database.

Go ahead, save your file, and run it.

database.php

{177}
```php
<?php
$conn = mysqli_connect("localhost","user","pw","siteusers");

if(mysqli_connect_errno()){
die("Connection to DB failed" .
mysqli_connect_error());
}
$uid = uniqid();
$username = "coinableS";
$addy = "1NPrfWgJfkANmd1jt88A141PjhiarT8d9U";

$addUser = "INSERT INTO siteusers (userid, username, address) VALUES('$uid', '$username', '$addy')";
$doAddUser = mysqli_query($conn, $addUser) or die(mysqli_error($conn));
?>
```

10.5 Fetching Data

Now that we have data in our table, we need to be able to fetch that data as well.

Let's start with a simple query to fetch the address that is associated with the username "coinableS".

{178}
```
$select = "SELECT * FROM siteusers WHERE username = 'coinableS'";
```

Our SQL statement tells it to check everything in the siteusers table where the username is "coinableS". Since we added this user in the last section, this should return with one row, and that row will include the user id, username, and address.

Now we need to execute the query, and then access the row returned to get the address for the user.

{179}
```
$doSelect = mysqli_query($conn, $select) or
die(mysqli_error($conn));
$fetchSelect = mysqli_fetch_assoc($doSelect);
$getAddy = $fetchSelect["address"];
```

Similar to the last section, we use `mysqli_query` to execute the command with `$conn` as our first parameter, and the variable with our SQL command in the second parameter.

Then we use `mysqli_fetch_assoc` to return the results of the query as an associative array. So at this point PHP now has an array under `$fetchSelect` that would look like this:

```
array(
  "userid"=>"us8213mn",
  "username"=>"coinableS",
  "address"=>"1NPrfWgJfkANmd1jt88A141PjhiarT8d9U"
);
```

So now we can grab any of those values we would like just as if it were a normal PHP array.

```
echo $fetchSelect["address"];
```

The above would print out the address.

```
echo $fetchSelect["userid"];
```

The above would print out the userid.
Or you can assign the value to a variable and then echo out the variable.

{180}
```
$getAddy = $fetchSelect["address"];
echo $getAddy;
```

The above would print out the address.

Go ahead, save your file, and run it. If everything is correct it will print out the address that corresponds to the username.

database.php
{181}
```
<?php
$conn = mysqli_connect("localhost","user","pw","siteusers");

if(mysqli_connect_errno()){
die("Connection to DB failed" .
mysqli_connect_error());
}
$select = "SELECT * FROM siteusers WHERE username =
'coinableS'";
$doSelect = mysqli_query($conn, $select) or
die(mysqli_error($conn));
$fetchSelect = mysqli_fetch_assoc($doSelect);
$getAddy = $fetchSelect["address"];
echo $getAddy;
?>
```

10.6 Updating Data

Now what if we wanted to change some data? Maybe the user has a balance stored on your database, and you want to update their balance.

In this example we will simply change the address associated with the username.

First let's create a variable with the new address we want to update to.

```
$newAddy = "1J9ikqFuwrzPbczsDkquA9uVYeq6dEehsj";
```

Then we'll create a SQL command that uses UPDATE and SET to change the address associated with the username "coinableS".

{182}
```
$updateAddy = "UPDATE siteusers SET address = 
'$newAddy' WHERE username='coinableS'";
$doUpdate = mysqli_query($conn, $updateAddy) or 
die(mysqli_error($conn));
```

You can now save this and run it to update the address.

database.php

{183}
```
<?php
$conn = mysqli_connect("localhost","user","pw","siteusers");

if(mysqli_connect_errno()){
die("Connection to DB failed" . 
mysqli_connect_error());
}
$newAddy = "1J9ikqFuwrzPbczsDkquA9uVYeq6dEehsj";
$updateAddy = "UPDATE siteusers SET address = 
'$newAddy' WHERE username='coinableS'";
$doUpdate = mysqli_query($conn, $updateAddy) or 
die(mysqli_error($conn));
echo "Table updated.";
?>
```

You can go back to the last section, and run the code that fetched the address, and it should now fetch the new address you just updated it to.

10.7 SQL Injection

At this point you should be able to see how powerful databases are, and how they make sites dynamic for each individual user. Not only are they powerful, but they can be dangerous when allowing users to input data in your tables.

Some malicious users will try to execute SQL code that will harm, or bypass security in your site known as SQL injection.

Please make sure you take the necessary steps in securing your site from SQL injection by escaping user inputs, or by using prepared statements or PDO.

I strongly suggest you do your own research into preventing SQL injection, and deciding which method is best for you. Prepared statements with PDO is very popular, however requires you to use Object Oriented Programming, which is different than the Procedural Style I am demonstrating in this book. PDO is one way to do it, but it's not the only way. You can successfully prevent SQL injection using Procedural Style as well. One of the great things about PHP is you can choose if you want to be an Object Oriented programmer or a Procedural Style programmer.

Let's take a look at a way to prevent SQL injection in a procedural style.

When accepting user inputted data, it will typically come in through a form on your website under the POST method. In PHP it would look something like this:

```
$username = $_POST["uname"];
```

Where "uname" is the name of the input form in the HTML form.

Unsafe Insert:

```
$username = $_POST["uname"];
$insert = "INSERT INTO table (username) VALUES ('$username')";
```

The above does nothing to prevent a malicious user. If you were to insert this directly into your database, you are open to SQL injection.

Instead we should escape the users input using `mysqli_real_escape_string();` this will remove unnecessary and potentially harmful characters like ", '.

Better Insert:

```
$username = $_POST["uname"];
$username = mysqli_real_escape_string($conn, $username);
$insert = "INSERT INTO table (username) VALUES ('$username')";
```

You can take it a step further by declaring the character set as well. Some characters in one charset can be interpreted differently in another charset. Some malicious users use this to their advantage to try to circumvent escaping strings.

Preferred Insert:

```
mysqli_set_charset($conn,"utf8");
$username = $_POST["uname"];
$username = mysqli_real_escape_string($conn, $username);
```

```
$insert = "INSERT INTO table (username) VALUES
('$username')";
```

In the above example we declare our charset as UTF-8.

This should keep you relatively safe. Keep in mind hackers are usually way ahead of developers, so it's best to think that anything you create can and might be hacked. So balance your risk by backing up your site, and databases regularly. Also if operating with live bitcoins on your site, keep the balance in your hot wallet down to a minimum. That way if you are hacked, your losses are reduced.

11. Version Control - Git

You might be wondering why I am going over Git, and let me say if you have ever used ctrl+Z you will want to use Git. The reason is if you go on with your web development adventure there will be a time when you will want to go back to how your site was a certain time in the past. Maybe you made a change that you didn't notice until a week and many saves later that you messed something up. With Git you can easily go back to how your site was without having to re-write all of your code.

Git let's you keep track of changes, file history, and different versions for a software project. Instead of having to re-name all your files Git will do the hard parts for you. For example if you have a file and name it new_file.php. Then you decide to add something to it, but you still want to keep new_file.php because you might want to go back, and use the code from it. Typically people will do something like new_file2.php. Great, there's an endless number of numbers, so this is a great plan, right? Well what happens when you get to new_file231.php and you want to go back to when you changed your menu schematic. Was that new_file201 or new_file102? This is where Git comes in handy.

11.1 Download and Install Git

In order to use Git you'll need to download the software. Do a web search for "download Git". As of this writing, Git is hosted as git-scm.com. Click on the download section and download Git.

Locate the installer file that you just downloaded, and follow the installation instructions, just keep all the defaults. You will want to select the section that has Git Bash, which is a linux style command-line version that you can use.

After install, locate the directory that you installed Git to, and launch the Git Bash application. You should see something like:

Great looks like it worked! For your first command type in:

```
git help
```

Hit enter and it should provide you with some commands that are available for use and what they do.

```
$ git help
usage: git [--version] [--help] [-C <path>] [-c name=value]
           [--exec-path[=<path>]] [--html-path] [--man-path] [--info-path]
           [-p|--paginate|--no-pager] [--no-replace-objects] [--bare]
           [--git-dir=<path>] [--work-tree=<path>] [--namespace=<name>]
           <command> [<args>]

The most commonly used git commands are:
   add        Add file contents to the index
   bisect     Find by binary search the change that introduced a bug
   branch     List, create, or delete branches
   checkout   Checkout a branch or paths to the working tree
   clone      Clone a repository into a new directory
   commit     Record changes to the repository
   diff       Show changes between commits, commit and working tree, etc
   fetch      Download objects and refs from another repository
   grep       Print lines matching a pattern
   init       Create an empty Git repository or reinitialize an existing one
   log        Show commit logs
   merge      Join two or more development histories together
   mv         Move or rename a file, a directory, or a symlink
   pull       Fetch from and integrate with another repository or a local branch
   push       Update remote refs along with associated objects
   rebase     Forward-port local commits to the updated upstream head
   reset      Reset current HEAD to the specified state
   rm         Remove files from the working tree and from the index
   show       Show various types of objects
   status     Show the working tree status
   tag        Create, list, delete or verify a tag object signed with GPG

'git help -a' and 'git help -g' lists available subcommands and some
concept guides. See 'git help <command>' or 'git help <concept>'
to read about a specific subcommand or concept.
```

11.2 Account Configuration

Now we need to set up our username. Within the Git bash window type in

```
git config -global user.name "Kyle"
```

I put in Kyle, but you should make up your own username. You can verify that your username was set by typing: git config user.name

We can also set our email address to link with the username, by typing.

```
git config -global user.email "satoshi@bitcoin.org"
```

You can verify your email was set with your user name by typing

```
git config -list
```

11.3 Creating An Example Git Project

We will begin by creating a new empty folder, you can just put it on the desktop, and name it anything. This folder will be targeted by Git as the project folder, and once initialized it will begin to manage changes within that folder.

Now we need to navigate to the folder. Sure you can just open the folder, and then right-click to open the Git bash there, but let's manually navigate using Linux command-line.

Go back to your Git bash, and change to your home directory:

```
cd ~
```

Now, change directories to your desktop

```
cd desktop
```

Great, now let's move the the New Project folder, mind the SPACE!

```
cd "New Project"
```

Then if you type in `pwd` for print working directory it should tell you that you are in the New Project folder on your desktop.

```
Kyle@SATELLITE ~/desktop/New Project
$ cd ~

Kyle@SATELLITE ~
$ cd desktop

Kyle@SATELLITE ~/desktop
$ cd "New Project"

Kyle@SATELLITE ~/desktop/New Project
$ pwd
/c/Users/Kyle/desktop/New Project
```

Now that we know we are in the correct folder, let's make this folder a Git project.

Type `git init` meaning initiate Git in this folder

```
git init
```

It should respond with "Initialized empty Git repository in C:/..."

Now you have created your first Git repository!

11.4 Committing a File

Now that we have created our repository in our New Project folder, it is time to add a file so we can see how things work.

Start a new text file, write something in the file, and save it inside the New Project folder. I created a file called test.txt and the content reads "There can only be 21 billion bitcoins."

Now go into our Git bash command-line, and add the file to the Git repository.

```
git add test.txt
```

You can also tell Git to add all files by using

```
git add .
```

If you want to see more options with `git add` type in `git add -help`

Now that we have added the file we need to commit it to our repository, and add a descriptive message about the commit. This way when you have 20+ commits you will know what this specific commit changed, so if you wanted to you can go back to it at a later time.

```
git commit -m "Initial commit"
```

```
Kyle@SATELLITE ~/desktop/New Project (master)
$ git add test.txt
Kyle@SATELLITE ~/desktop/New Project (master)
$ git commit -m "Inital commit"
[master (root-commit) ab846ec] Inital commit
 1 file changed, 1 insertion(+)
 create mode 100644 test.txt
```

Awesome, you just made your very first Git commit! Now we'll know that this is our very first commit to our project.

11.5 Making Changes

Let's go back to our text file, and make a change. I'm going to fix my initial text file because I stated 21 billion bitcoins, but it should be 21 million. So I'll make the change and save it.

Now I need to commit this change to the repository.

First add the file, then commit it.

```
git add test.txt
git commit -m "21 billion to 21 million"
```

Now I will know exactly what this change was for. You can check your commit logs by typing

```
git log
```

```
Kyle@SATELLITE ~/desktop/New Project (master)
$ git log
commit df78029cb88c19721338048e5a5f7c328e20ced0
Author: Kyle <coinables@gmail.com>
Date:   Sat Mar 19 21:59:18 2016 -0700

    21 billion to 21 million

commit ab846eca781c3cb3c609a844046a8d88b13869b5
Author: Kyle <coinables@gmail.com>
Date:   Sat Mar 19 21:54:07 2016 -0700

    Inital commit
```

Here you can see that I have so far made two commits, one was the initial, and the other was to change billion to million.

But what if you made a change to a file or maybe you don't remember if you made a change since your last commit. You can check to see if your working files match your Git repository by typing `git status`.

If there are no changes you should see "Nothing to commit, working directory clean".

If you do have any changes that are not committed, or not matching your repository it will tell you changes are not staged.

```
Kyle@SATELLITE ~/desktop/New Project (master)
$ git status
On branch master
Changes not staged for commit:
  (use "git add <file>..." to update what will be
  (use "git checkout -- <file>..." to discard chan

        modified:   test.txt

no changes added to commit (use "git add" and/or
```

Go ahead and make some changes to your text file, and make a few commits. Now let's revert back to an older version of our file.

First use Git log to see your previous commits.

```
Kyle@SATELLITE ~/desktop/New Project (master)
$ git log
commit 3413b5e0d26975aff541ff36abf69249e5b19936
Author: Kyle <coinables@gmail.com>
Date:   Sat Mar 19 22:15:38 2016 -0700

    Included Satoshi Nakamoto

commit 13fc5d2c43ff4ba65b9e3912d15691cceeaeb5ff
Author: Kyle <coinables@gmail.com>
Date:   Sat Mar 19 22:14:39 2016 -0700

    Added Neat at the end

commit df78029cb88c19721338048e5a5f7c328e20ced0
Author: Kyle <coinables@gmail.com>
Date:   Sat Mar 19 21:59:18 2016 -0700

    21 billion to 21 million

commit ab846eca781c3cb3c609a844046a8d88b13869b5
Author: Kyle <coinables@gmail.com>
Date:   Sat Mar 19 21:54:07 2016 -0700

    Inital commit
```

We need to reference the commit identifier of the one we want to go back to. So in order to go back to the commit where I change billion to million I need to reference df78029cb88c19721338048e5a5f7c328e20ced0, but that is really long. Good thing we only need to type in the first few characters for it to work.

Let's bring back that old copy using Git checkout

```
git checkout df7802 -- test.txt
```

Now our working copy inside our New Project folder will be back to how it was when we committed the 21 billion to 21 million change. Awesome!

Since this is just a change with our working copy file, we need to commit it.

```
git add test.txt

git commit -m "reverted back to 21 billion commit"
```

```
Kyle@SATELLITE ~/desktop/New Project (master)
$ git checkout df7802 -- test.txt

Kyle@SATELLITE ~/desktop/New Project (master)
$ git add test.txt

Kyle@SATELLITE ~/desktop/New Project (master)
$ git commit -m "reverted back to 21 million commit"
[master a7f7e21] reverted back to 21 million commit
 1 file changed, 1 insertion(+), 1 deletion(-)
```

Pretty cool, huh? This was just a basic introduction to Git, there are a lot more features that I did not go over. Branching is a very useful way to have multiple versions of your project going at a time. I encourage you to take the time and learn more of Git's features https://git-scm.com/doc

It's great to get in the habit of using Git with your projects. If you are able to make it a habit you will not regret it. Every developer runs into a situation where they wish they could go back to an older version. Git can save you time and headaches. It's no fun having to re-write an entire project.

12. PROJECT: Build a Basic E-Commerce Site

Congratulations! You have made it to the end of the book! You now have some of the basic knowledge required to start building your own bitcoin websites from scratch. This is the part where I will go over some creation processes and provide working examples that you can use.

For this project we are going to create a simple site where you can sell goods for bitcoin. It's not meant to be an Amazon, it's meant to be for a small business who wants to sell their own items online for bitcoin. We are going to accomplish this by using a 3rd Party API, so if you did not read Chapter 8, I suggest you go back and do so now.

12.1 Layout and Build

I know the title is easier said than done, but this part just takes time. Come up with a layout that you want to use just using HTML and CSS.

Plan ahead! Think about what your site will need, and the stages that a shopper will take. It's best to get out a pencil and paper and start sketching your basic layout, and make notes about what sort of PHP code you will need to make the store come alive.

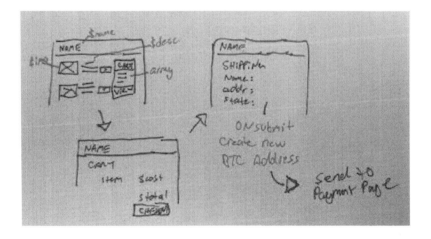

The basic schematic we are going to use for this project will be a main page, a separate page for each product, a checkout page to collect order information, and lastly a payment page. Below is a visual representation of the site map.

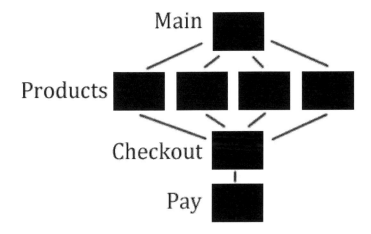

12.2 Create the Main Page

This part you can get as creative as you want with styling, colors, images, etc. In my example I will keep it very basic leaving most of the styling up to you.

We should have a header with the store name, a description area to explain your store to the user, and a list of products. Of course you can have more, but this should be considered a minimum requirement.

For the header we will create a `<div>` at the top of the page, and then give it some parameters in CSS.

CSS:
```
#banner{
   background-color: #00ccff;
   font-size: 30px;
}
```

HTML:
```html
<div id="banner">Shop Name</div>
```

Then we'll add a short description below the header. You can put it in a `<div>` but for this example I'm just going to stick it in paragraph tag.

```html
<p> Enter shop description here. This is a basic example of a bitcoin ecommerce site. This solution is intended for small shops with few products. </p>
```

Under our description we can start inserting our products. Include the name of the product, the price, a small image and a link.

Each product will have a link to it's own unique PHP page. So if you have 3 items for sale, you will have 3 different PHP pages to link to. Let's call these item pages, the first item page will be item1.php, the second will be item2.php, and so on.

Example with three items:
CSS:
{184}
```css
.pr {
        border: 1px solid #666666;
        border-radius: 3px;
}
```

HTML:
{185}
```html
<h2>Latest Items For Sale</h2>
<table>
<tr>
<td class="pr"><center>Item 1 $20<br>
<img src="images/item1.jpg"><br>
<a href="item1.php">Buy Now!</a>
</center></td>

<td class="pr"><center>Item 2 $30<br>
<img src="images/item2.jpg"><br>
```

```
<a href="item2.php">Buy Now!</a>
</center></td>

<td class="pr"><center>Item 3 $50<br>
<img src="images/item3.jpg"><br>
<a href="item3.php">Buy Now!</a>
</center></td>
</tr>
</table>
```

12.3 Create the Product Pages

The product pages will contain some more information about the product, possibly more images of the product, and most importantly a buy button that will take the user to a checkout page.

This page will need to be a PHP page because we will need to fetch the current exchange rate and convert it to the USD amount we are charging for our product.

Below is an example using BTC-e as the exchange rate. We will round the decimal places down to four to make it more friendly to consumers. A shopper doesn't want to see "Please send 0.01663542 BTC", it's confusing, inconvenient, and really unnecessary. Changing that to 0.0166 is much easier to read, and is still accurate down to 10,000 satoshis or five cents if one bitcoin is worth $500.

PHP:

{186}
```
<?php
$url = "https://btc-e.com/api/2/btc_usd/ticker";
$json = json_decode(file_get_contents($url), true);
$price = $json["ticker"]["last"];
$usdPrice = 20; // SET THE PRICE OF THE ITEM HERE
$calc = $usdPrice / $price;
$itemPrice = round($calc, 4);
?>
```

Now we can include the bitcoin price in our HTML just by inserting some PHP tags and echoing `$itemPrice`.

The buy button will need to relay which item the customer is going to purchase. We can add an identifier to the Buy Now link (checkout.php?item=1) using what is known as a GET.

CSS:

{187}
```
.btn{
  padding: 8px;
  padding-left: 16px;
  padding-right: 16px;
  border: 1px solid #ccc;
  border-radius: 5px;
  text-decoration: none;
  color: #666;
  font-weight: strong;
}
```

HTML:

{188}
```
<table width="80%">
<tr>
  <td width="40%">
  <img src="images/item1.jpg" width="95%"></td>
  <td width="60%">
  <h2>Item 1 Title</h2>
  <br><br>
  <h3>$20.00</h3>
  <h3><?php echo $itemPrice; ?>BTC</h3>
  <br>
  <a class="btn" href="checkout.php?item=1">Buy Now</a>
  </td>
</tr>
<tr>
<td colspan="2">Additional longer description of the item will go here.</td>
</tr>
</table>
```

That should do it! Now you just need to create an item2.php using the same code, but just change `$usdPrice` variable, the images, and description in the HTML. You will need create additional item#.php pages for every item you want to sell on your site.

12.4 Create the Checkout Page

The checkout page will ask the customer for their contact information so you can ship them the product you are selling. For this we will need to create a simple form.

Create a new form using the `<form>` tags, set the method equal to post and action equal to pay.php.

```
<form method="post" action="pay.php">
</form>
```

Inside the form tags, use `<input>` tags for the user to enter their data. Set the type as text, and for each input we will need a name property that has a unique value. This part is important as it is how we will grab the data from the form and use it in our PHP code.

```
Name: <input type="text" name="name"><br>
Address: <input type="text" name="street"><br>
```

Once you have created all the input fields that you want on your customer, we will need to create a submit button to submit the form. We will use the `<input>` tag again but this time with the type equal to submit, and it will also need a unique name property.

```
<input type="submit" name="checkout" value="Proceed to Payment">
```

The value property is how the button will read to the customer, in this case the button will say "Proceed to Payment".

Remember how we put that identifier in the link on the product page? We'll use PHP to grab that information so we know which item the customer is purchasing.

Getting information from the URL, known as a GET request, is simple in PHP. All you do is use `$_GET[""];` and then inside the quotes enter in the parameter name, in our case we used the name "item". So to assign that value to a variable we would just do:

```
$item = $_GET["item"];
```

Now we have item number from the URL stored in the variable `$item`. We can take this a step further and use a switch statement to change the cost and product name based on the value in the GET.

{189}
```
switch($item){
      case 1:
         $cost = 20;
         $product = "Item 1";
      break;
      case 2:
         $cost = 30;
         $product = "Item 2";
      break;
      case 3:
         $cost = 50;
         $product = "Item 3";
      break;
}
```

The above switch statement says that if the `$item` variable is equal to 1, then the `$cost` will be 20, and the `$product` will have the name of "Item 1".

We can then drop that into the top of the HTML portion of the checkout page, so the user knows that they are checking out for the right item.

```
You selected to buy <?php echo $product; ?>
```

Now we need to get that switch to carry over to the payment page. We can include in our `$_POST` as a hidden input `<input type="hidden" value="<?php echo $cost; ?>">`. But that can create bad habits, since malicious users can edit POST variables. What we can do instead is put the values into `$_SESSION` variables.

After your switch, start the session.

```
session_start();
```

Then create a new session variable for the product and the cost so it can be used on the payment page.

```
$_SESSION["product"] = $product;
$_SESSION["cost"] = $cost;
```

Now these can be carried over to our next page, the payment page.

12.5 Creating the Payment Page

This is where the fun starts. The payment page will do several things including: generate a new address for receiving payment, create a QR code to prompt the user to send the payment, and send an email to both the user and ourselves so we can be notified of the new order.

I would suggest displaying the users contact information they just entered so they can verify they entered the correct information before sending payment.

The first thing we need to do is start the session so we can use the session variables we created on the last page.

```
<?php
session_start();
?>
```

We can then output both the session and post variables to the page.

```
<?php
session_start();
?>
<html>
Order Details:<br>
Item: <?php echo $_SESSION['product']; ?><br>
Cost: <?php echo $_SESSION['cost']; ?><br>
Name: <?php echo $_POST['name']; ?><br>
Address: <?php echo $_POST['street']; ?><br>
</html>
```

PRO TIP: It's not a good idea to display user's POST content to a page without stripping it first. In this case it is fine because this data only displays back to the user within their session only. If it were going to be posted on a public page that others could see then this opens your site to XSS(cross-site scripting). You can mitigate these types of attacks using `htmlspecialchars($some_variable);`

Now we can create a new address to receive payment using Blockchain.info Receive Payments API. See Chapter 8.

{191}
```php
<?php
session_start();
$api_key = "your_blockchain_api_Key";
$xpub = "xpubYour_extended_public_key";
$secret = "your_secret"; //this can be anything you want
$rootURL = "http://yourrooturl.com/directory";
$orderID = uniqid();

$callback_url = $rootURL."/callback.php?invoice=".$orderID."&secret=".$secret;
$receive_url = "https://api.blockchain.info/v2/receive?key=".$api_key."&xpub=".$xpub."&callback=".urlencode($callback_url);
$ch = curl_init();
curl_setopt($ch, CURLOPT_SSL_VERIFYPEER, true);
curl_setopt($ch, CURLOPT_RETURNTRANSFER, true);
curl_setopt($ch, CURLOPT_URL, $receive_url);
$ccc = curl_exec($ch);
$json = json_decode($ccc, true);
$payTo = $json['address'];
?>
```

The new receiving address is now stored under the `$payTo` variable. If you want you can just put the address on the screen, but we should also calculate the payment in bitcoin and give the user a QR code so they can scan it with their cell phone.

Calculate the payment using the session variable of cost just like we did earlier on the product page.

{192}
```php
$url = "https://btc-e.com/api/2/btc_usd/ticker";
$json = json_decode(file_get_contents($url), true);
$price = $json["ticker"]["last"];
$usdPrice = $_SESSION['cost'];
$calc = $usdPrice / $price;
$itemPrice = round($calc, 4);
```

Use Google's Chart API to create a QR code.

{193}
```html
<img src="http://chart.googleapis.com/chart?chs=125x125&cht=qr&chl=<?php echo $payTo; ?>" width="50%">
```

It's just a call to an image file where we can insert the Bitcoin address in the `chl` property.

Then we'll use PHP's `mail();` function to notify ourselves of the order and email the customer a confirmation email. Hopefully one of your input boxes from the checkout page was the users' email address ;)

{194}
```php
$host = $_SERVER['SERVER_NAME'];
$headers = "From: noreply@".$host."\r\n";
$headers .= "Content-type: text/html\r\n";
//customer email
$email = $_POST['customer_email'];
$emailTitle_Customer = "Order Confirmation #".$orderID;
$customerEmail = <<<EOD
    <h3>Please send payment to finalize your purchase</h3>
    Payment Address: $payTo <br>
    Payment Amount: $itemPrice <br>
EOD;
    $customerCopy = mail($email, $emailTitle_Customer, $customerEmail, $headers);
//merchant email
```

```
$yourEmail = "your@email.com";
$emailTitle = "New Order";
$bodyEmail = <<<EOD
    <h1>New Purchase</h1>
    Order: $orderID <br>
    Email: $email <br>
    Name: $name <br>
    Address: $address <br>
    Payment Address: $payTo <br>
    Payment Amount: $itemPrice <br>
EOD;
    $ourCopy = mail("$yourEmail", "$emailTitle",
"$bodyEmail", "$headers");
```

Let's go over a few things to point out in the above block of code for the email.

First, `$host`, this is set equal to the domain name of our website which will do so automatically when calling `$_SERVER['SERVER_NAME'];`

The `$headers` variable sets the headers for the email, we basically tell it that the content is text and HTML. We also set who the email is sent from in the headers, in this example we have it sent from noreply@ your domain name.

The `<<<EOD` you see is known as HEREDOC and is quick way to write multi-line strings. You can go in and out of HTML and PHP without having to use a bunch of (.) and ("). The HEREDOC portion ends with `EOD;`.

Lastly is the `mail()` function itself. The schematic it works off of is `mail($to, $subject, $body, $headers)` in this order.

At this point the rest is up to you. You can do what you wish with the callback.php page, again see Chapter 8 Receive Payments API for reference. Maybe you want it to update a database or send you an email that the user has made the payment, it's all up to you!

Checkout Blockchain Receive Payments API Shopping Cart project on my GitHub. It's a more advanced version of this, but also uses a database, websocket, and has an admin section for easy adding and removing products.

https://github.com/coinables/Blockchain-Receive-Payments-API-Shopping-Cart

13. PROJECT: Build a Simple Game (JSON-RPC)

DISCLAIMER: PLEASE BE AWARE OF YOUR LOCAL AND INTERNATIONAL GAMING LAWS. IF YOU BUILD AN ILLEGAL BITCOIN GAMBLING SITE YOU WILL LIKELY END UP IN PRISON.

Since this chapter alone could be an entire book, I'm going to keep this as simple as possible and create a very basic guessing game that rewards correct guesses with bitcoin.

13.1 Create the Database

Our database will need a users table, and a games table. The users table should have a USERID, USERNAME, PASSWORD, DEPOSIT_ADDRESS, and BALANCE. The games table should have GAMEID, PLAYER, TARGET, GUESS, and OPEN. Please reference Chapter 10 if you need help with creating a database.

Users Table schematic:
USERID : varchar(20) : Primary Key : *A unique ID*
USERNAME : varchar(20) : *The players username*
PASSWORD : varchar(200) : *Hashed password*
DEPOSIT_ADDRESS : varchar(50) : *Bitcoin address*
BALANCE : integer(12) : *Users bitcoin balance*

Games Table schematic:
GAMEID : integer(20) auto-increment : Primary Key : *Game ID*
PLAYER : varchar(20) : *UserID of player for this round*
TARGET : integer(3) : *The number the user will try to guess*
GUESS : integer(1) : *The user's guess*
WINLOSE: integer(1) : *Outcome of the game*

That's it! Remember, I said simple example.

PRO TIP: When creating tables and the column names please be aware that there are certain reserved words by mysql, words like PASSWORD. If you choose to use a reserved word like I did you just need to make sure to wrap it in back-tics ` `. Note these are different than ' or ".

13.2 Create the Registration Page

Before a user can play they will need to create an account with a password. You should encourage your users to use strong passwords and not to repeat passwords across multiple sites.

Create a simple form with a username field, a password field and a verify password field. So you will end up with three input boxes and a submit button.

{195}
```
<form method="post">
Username:<br> <input type="text" id="username"
name="username" maxlength="20"><br>
Password:<br> <input type="password" id="pw"
name="pw"><br>
Retype Password:<br> <input type="password" id="pw2"
name="pw2"><br>
<input type="submit" name="submit" value="REGISTER" />
</form>
```

In the PHP portion, other than connecting to your database, we'll want to check a few things, sanitize the inputs, and hash the password before inputting it to our database.

Sanitize inputs and hash the password:

{196}
```
$username = $_POST['username'];
$password = $_POST['pw'];
$password2 = $_POST['pw2'];


mysqli_set_charset($conn,"utf8");
$username = mysqli_real_escape_string($conn,
$username);
$password = mysqli_real_escape_string($conn,
$password);
$password2 = mysqli_real_escape_string($conn,
$password2);
$salt = "abc123";
$enc_pass = hash_hmac("sha384", $salt, $password);
```

PRO TIP: Hashing passwords is crucial to proper site management. If your site is ever compromised you don't want the attacker to get your users passwords. Hashing the password with a salt(random string) will prevent an attacker from decrypting the passwords.

Check if inputs are empty and if passwords match.

{197}
```
if(trim($_POST['username'])==''){
 $message = "You must enter a name";
}
else if(trim($_POST['pw']) ==''){
$message = "You must enter a password";
}
else if ($password != $password2){
$message = "Passwords Do Not Match";
}
```

Check to see if the username already exists. Query the database to select everything from the users table where USERNAME equals the username variable and count the number of rows returned.

{198}
```
$dupName = mysqli_query($conn, "SELECT * FROM users WHERE USERNAME = '$username'");
$rowName = mysqli_num_rows($dupName);
```

Then see if the number of rows returned does not equal zero. If it does not equal zero, then the username is already in use.

{199}
```
if ($rowName != 0) {
$message = "Username is already in use, pick another";
}
```

If all pass, then we can create a unique ID for the user, a deposit address for them to use and insert the data into the database. See chapter 9 for creating new addresses using Bitcoin JSON-RPC.

{200}
```
$userid = uniqid();
$bitcoin = new Bitcoin("username", "somepassword");
$addy = $bitcoin->getnewaddress();
$newuser = "INSERT INTO users
(USERID, USERNAME, `PASSWORD`, DEPOSIT_ADDRESS,
BALANCE)
VALUES ('$userid', '$username', '$enc_pass', '$addy',
0)";
$newuserQuery = mysqli_query($conn, $newuser);
```

Don't forget to back-tic the PASSWORD column since it is a reserved name in MySQL.

After we insert the new user to the database, we can start a new session and move them to the game page.

{201}
```
session_start();
$_SESSION['nuid'] = $userid;
header('Location: https://yoursite.com/game.php');
```

13.3 Create a Log In Page

We will also need to create a login page for returning users. This will be easy since we already have most of it created from the registration page.

We can use the same HTML form, but remove the 2nd password field and change the name of the submit button from Register to LogIn.

{202}
```
<form method="post">
Username:<br> <input type="text" id="username" name="username" maxlength="20"><br>
Password:<br> <input type="password" id="pw" name="pw"><br>
<input type="submit" name="submit" value="LOGIN" />
</form>
```

We'll do the same sanitation as the registration page, but our SQL will check where both username and hashed password matches the database.

{203}
```
$username = $_POST['username'];
$password = $_POST['pw'];

mysqli_set_charset($conn,"utf8");
$username = mysqli_real_escape_string($conn, $username);
$password = mysqli_real_escape_string($conn, $password);
$salt = "abc123";
$enc_pass = hash_hmac("sha384", $salt, $password);

$loginCheck = mysqli_query($conn, "SELECT * FROM users WHERE USERNAME = '$username' AND `PASSWORD` = '$enc_pass'");
$rowLogin = mysqli_num_rows($loginCheck);
```

Then we check for the number of rows returned. If there is a row returned then we have a successful login. At that point we'll pull the corresponding userID, start a new session and move them to the game page.

{204}
```
if ($rowLogin == 1) {
$getuid = mysqli_fetch_assoc($loginCheck);
$userid = $getuid["USERID"];
session_start();
$_SESSION['nuid'] = $userid;
header('Location: https://yoursite.com/game.php');
}
```

13.4 Creating the Game Page

The very first thing we need to do on the game page, is make sure the user is actually logged in and not trying to manually navigate the user page.

Start the session, and grab the userID from the session variable we created on the previous page. If they are not in a valid session or the user ID within the variable does not exist then we send the user directly back to the login page.

{205}
```
$userid = $_SESSION['nuid'];
$trueLogin = "SELECT * FROM users WHERE USERID = '$userid'";
$doTrueLogin = mysqli_query($conn, $trueLogin);
$rowsTrueLogin = mysqli_num_rows($doTrueLogin);
if($rowsTrueLogin != 1){
header("Location: login.php");
}
```

Now we can use the userid to grab their current balance and deposit address so they can send some funds to play with.

{206}
```
$userData = "SELECT * FROM users WHERE USERID = '$userid'";
$doUserData = mysqli_query($conn, $userData);
$fetchUserData = mysqli_fetch_assoc($doUserData);
$balance = $fetchUserData["BALANCE"];
$deposit_address = $fetchUserData["DEPOSIT_ADDRESS"];
```

On the HTML side, let's greet the user by their username and show them their balance and where to send a deposit.

{207}
```
<h4>Welcome, <?php echo $username; ?></h4><br>
Your Balance: <?php echo $balance; ?><br>
```

```
Deposit Address: <?php echo $deposit_address; ?><br>
<img src="http://chart.googleapis.com/chart?
chs=125x125&cht=qr&chl=<?php echo $deposit_address; ?>
">
```

The last line is using Google's Chart API to create a QR code of the deposit address, just as we did in our last chapter.

13.5 Building the Game Code

This part is where we come up with the rules for the game we want to create. The example I will use for this project will allow a user to guess if the computer will pick a number greater than or less than 50. The computer will randomly select a number between 1 and 100. To keep things extra simple we will not allow the user to input any data, just click a button.

First let's create the form that the user will use to make their guesses. We can put it below the greeting with their balance and deposit address.

{208}
```
<hr>
RULES: The object of the game is to correctly guess if
the computer will pick a number greater than or less
than 50.
Every guess will cost you 100 satoshis. If you guess
correctly you will win 198 satoshis in return, if you
guess wrong you receive nothing. BONUS, if you guess
correctly with the EXACTLY 50 option you will win 9,900
satoshis. <br>
<h4>Make your guess!</h4>
<form method="post">
<input type="submit" name="greater" value="OVER
50"><br>
<input type="submit" name="less" value="UNDER 50"><br>
<input type="submit" name="exact" value="EXACTLY
50"><br>
</form>
```

In the above example we also added a button the user can use to guess the number will be exactly 50, and if they are correct they will win 99x the cost.

This is where the house edge is created. The house edge is a probability factor where on a statistical average the website owner, you, should win more often than the player. For example the user has a 1 in 100 chance of getting the "Exactly 50" option correct, but they only win 99x if they are correct, this creates a 1% house edge.

That's basically it for the HTML side, now let's build the back-end in PHP.

When the page is initially loaded we immediately have the computer pick a number between 1 and 100 using `mt_rand();`.

`$winningNumber = mt_rand(1,100);`

Well that was easy! Now we can create three different isset `$_POST` combinations, one for each possible selection the user can make. You could also use a switch statement if you're feeling confident!

Here's what the greater than option will look like.

{209}
```
if(isset($_POST['greater']))
{
   //check if they have enough to play
   if($balance < 100){
      $message = "You need at least 100 satoshi to play";
   } else {
```

```php
    $guess = 1;
    if($winningNumber > 50)
    {
    //user wins
    $message = "You Win! +99 Satoshis";
    $message .= "<br> The computer picked ". $winningNumber;
    $winlose = 1;
    $insertGame = "INSERT INTO games (PLAYER, TARGET, GUESS, WINLOSE) VALUES ('$userid', '$winningNumber', '$guess', '$winlose')";
    $doInsertGame = mysqli_query($conn, $insertGame) or die(mysqli_error($conn));
    $updateBalance = "UPDATE users SET BALANCE = BALANCE + 99 WHERE USERID = '$userid'";
    $doUpdateBalance = mysqli_query($conn, $updateBalance);
    //get balance
    $userData = "SELECT * FROM users WHERE USERID = '$userid'";
    $doUserData = mysqli_query($conn, $userData);
    $fetchUserData = mysqli_fetch_assoc($doUserData);
    $balance = $fetchUserData["BALANCE"];
    } else
    {
    //user loses
    $message = "You Lose! -100 Satoshis";
    $message .= "<br> The computer picked ". $winningNumber;
    $winlose = 0;
    $insertGame = "INSERT INTO games (PLAYER, TARGET, GUESS, WINLOSE) VALUES ('$userid', '$winningNumber', '$guess', '$winlose')";
    $doInsertGame = mysqli_query($conn, $insertGame) or die(mysqli_error($conn));
    $updateBalance = "UPDATE users SET BALANCE = BALANCE - 100 WHERE USERID = '$userid'";
    $doUpdateBalance = mysqli_query($conn, $updateBalance);
    //get balance
    $userData = "SELECT * FROM users WHERE USERID = '$userid'";
    $doUserData = mysqli_query($conn, $userData);
    $fetchUserData = mysqli_fetch_assoc($doUserData);
    $balance = $fetchUserData["BALANCE"];
    }
  }
}
```

You should be able to use the above example for the "greater than" choice to build out the rest of the game. Just by making some simple changes like:

Changing this:

```
if($winningNumber > 50)
```

To this:

```
if($winningNumber < 50)
```

Or this:

```
if($winningNumber == 50)
```

And don't forget to change the reward amount on the Exactly 50 option

{210}
```
$updateBalance = "UPDATE users SET BALANCE = BALANCE + 9900 WHERE USERID = '$userid'";
$doUpdateBalance = mysqli_query($conn, $updateBalance);
```

We should also add a bit of code to the end of each isset post that pulls an updated balance from the database. If this part is left out then the balance will always be delayed by one game. We can literally copy and paste the code that we used before.

{211}
```
$userData = "SELECT * FROM users WHERE USERID = '$userid'";
$doUserData = mysqli_query($conn, $userData);
$fetchUserData = mysqli_fetch_assoc($doUserData);
$balance = $fetchUserData["BALANCE"];
```

We can simply add a logout button by redirecting the user to the login page and destroying the session.

{212}
```
if(isset($_POST['logout'])){
      session_destroy();
      header('Location: login');
      }
```

And the HTML for the logout button:

```
<input type="submit" name="logout" value="logout">
```

13.6 Processing Deposits

In order to credit funds to user accounts we will need to be able to check the blockchain for new transactions. We could do this by using the built-in feature walletnotify. Walletnotify will automatically fire anytime there is new activity on an address that is owned by your wallet.

Walletnotify needs to be defined in your bitcoin.conf file, example:

{213}
```
walletnotify = curl http://mysite.com/newdeposit.php?tx=%s
```

In the above example every time there is a new transaction on your wallet, the newdeposit.php page will run and the transaction ID will be stored in a GET named tx.

We could also do this by using the JSON-RPC call of `getreceivedbyaddress`, and calculate if there is a difference from the last time we checked. For example if our database has a previous received of 1 bitcoin and then we run `getreceivedbyaddress` and it returns 1.3 then we know that the balance should be increased by 0.3.

The `getreceivedbyaddress` method can be wasteful as it will execute a command to the node every time whether or not there has been a new transaction. If you have a lot of users this can drain resources.

Personally I think the best way to handle new deposits is by using walletnotify.

It would be wise not to name your page newdeposit.php I'm just using this as an example, it would be better use something unintelligible like 4bd29a841c.php. You don't want an attacker to be able to guess your deposit page.

Then we can pull the transaction id from the tx GET and put it through a gettransaction command.

{214}
```
$tx = $_GET['tx'];
$getTrans = $bitcoin->gettransaction($tx);
```

From there we need to look through the entire transaction, see if it has at least once confirmation, and how much was sent to the address in our wallet. We'll do this by running a loop, checking for the "receive" category and lastly compare the address to our database for a match. If there is a match we will update the balance for the account associated with the address.

{215}
```
$confirmations = $getTrans["confirmations"];
if($confirmations < 1){
die();
```

```
  } else {
    $countDetails = count($getTrans['details']);
    for($i=0;$i<$countDetails;$i++){
      $getAddress = $getTrans['details'][$i]['address'];
      $getReceive = $getTrans['details'][$i]['category'];
      if($getReceive == "receive"){
        $checkAddy = mysqli_query($conn, "SELECT * FROM users
WHERE DEPOSIT_ADDRESS = '$getAddress'");
        $doCheckAddy = mysqli_num_rows($checkAddy);
        if($doCheckAddy == 1){
        $amount = $getTrans['details'][$i]['amount'];
        $amount = $amount * 100000000;
        $updateBalance = "UPDATE users SET BALANCE = BALANCE +
'$amount' WHERE DEPOSIT_ADDRESS = '$getAddress'";
        $doUpdateBalance = mysqli_query($conn, $updateBalance);
        }
      }
    }
}
```

Walletnotify only fires twice. Once when the transaction first appears on the network, and a second time after it has been included in a block(one confirmation).

Don't forget to multiply the amount by 100 million to turn it into satoshis. Whole numbers are better for computers and databases to work with. Storing balances in decimal format is dangerous. PHP will try to convert decimals to things like 8.4E3.

There you go, that will be able to handle all incoming deposits.

13.7 Allowing Withdrawals

The withdrawal portion of your site will be the most targeted by attackers. If an attacker can exploit your withdrawal process they can wipe out your entire wallet, so it's best to focus more on security and less on convenience for the customer. Some sites process withdrawals manually, I think this is a bit too conservative, as it will require a lot of constant work to stay on top of withdrawals and it will greatly inconvenience customers.

For this example we will allow the user to input their Bitcoin address and nothing else. We don't want to give them the option to specify how much they can withdrawal. Now don't get confused by that last comment, you absolutely can allow them to specify an amount they want to withdrawal, but for this example we are not. It's easier and safer to withdrawal their full balance.

We can add a withdrawal button or link to our game page.

```
<input type="submit" name="withdrawal" value="Cash Out">
```

Add in the corresponding PHP code to re-direct them to a withdrawal page.

```
//withdrawal
if(isset($_POST['withdrawal'])){
      header('Location: withdrawal.php');
        }
```

Now we will create a new page named withdrawal.php. This page will check the database for the balance, confirm a user is still in a valid session and ask the user for their withdrawal address.

Confirm the user is logged in by counting the rows associated with their userid from the sessoin variable

{216}
```
$userid = $_SESSION['nuid'];
$trueLogin = "SELECT * FROM users WHERE USERID = '$userid'";
$doTrueLogin = mysqli_query($conn, $trueLogin);
$rowsTrueLogin = mysqli_num_rows($doTrueLogin);
if($rowsTrueLogin != 1){
```

```
//not logged in
header("Location: login.php");
} else
{
$userData = "SELECT * FROM users WHERE USERID = '$userid'";
$doUserData = mysqli_query($conn, $userData);
$fetchUserData = mysqli_fetch_assoc($doUserData);
$balance = $fetchUserData["BALANCE"];
$username = $fetchUserData["USERNAME"];
}
```

Then we added an else that will pull the users balance if they are in a legitimate session. You can copy this part straight from the game page we created.

Create a simple form that asks for the address they want to withdrawal to.

{217}
```
<form method="post">
Withdrawal to this Address: <input type="text" name="address" size="60"><br>
<input type="submit" name="withdrawal" value="Cash Out">
</form>
```

To make sure the user doesn't try anything fishy here, we should first validate what they entered is a valid address. Thankfully there is a built-in function with bitcoind that will do this called `validateaddress`.

`Validateaddress` will return more than just if it the address is valid, but also if the address belongs to your wallet and other information. Here's an example response from bitcoin.org's developer's reference guide.

```
{
    "isvalid" : true,
    "address" : "mgnucj8nYqdrPFh2JfZSB1NmUThUGnmsqe",
    "ismine" : true,
    "iswatchonly" : false,
    "isscript" : false,
```

```
    "pubkey" :
"03bacb84c6464a58b3e0a53cc0ba4cb3b82848cd7bed25a7724b3c
c75d76c9c1ba",
    "iscompressed" : true,
    "account" : "test label"
}
```

Notice the different information? We want to check the isvalid field. If it is not valid will return false. So we can assign the isvalid field to a variable, and then check if it is false by doing `if(!$variable)`, this basically says if variable doesn't exist or it returns false then do something. Here's an example:

{218}
```
if(isset($_POST['withdrawal'])){
$addy = trim($_POST['address']);
//validate
$checkAddy = $bitcoin->validateaddress($addy);
$isValid = $checkAddy['isvalid'];
        if(!$isValid){
           $message = "Address is invalid";
        } else {
        //process withdrawal
        }
}
```

Now let's update the if statement to include the actual withdrawal using `sendtoaddress`.

{219}
```
$convertBalance = $balance / 100000000;
$convertBalance = number_format($convertBalance, 8);
$doWithdrawal = $bitcoin->sendtoaddress($addy,
$convertBalance);
```

Remember that we store the balances in satoshis as integers in our database, so we have to convert it back to full bitcoins by dividing by 100 million. On smaller amounts like 1200, if we divide this by 100 million PHP will output 1.2E-5 instead of 0.000012, so we will also tell PHP to use 8 decimals by using `number_format()`.

Lastly we need to update the users balance back to zero, otherwise they could just keep withdrawing over-and-over.

{220}
```
$updateBalance = "UPDATE users SET BALANCE = 0 WHERE USERID = '$userid'";
$doUpdateBalance = mysqli_query($conn, $updateBalance);
```

It could also be beneficial to check the users balance, and if it is zero or less than a specific amount prevent them from withdrawing. This will prevent the user from sending commands to the bitcoin server requesting withdrawals of zero.

{221}
```
if(isset($_POST['withdrawal'])){

$addy = trim($_POST['address']);
//validate
$checkAddy = $bitcoin->validateaddress($addy);
$isValid = $checkAddy['isvalid'];
  if($balance < 1000){
  $message = "You need at least 1000 to withdrawal";
  } else {
    if(!$isValid){
    $message = "Address is invalid";
    } else {
    //process withdrawal
    $convertBalance = $balance / 100000000;
    $convertBalance = number_format($convertBalance, 8);
    $doWithdrawal = $bitcoin->sendtoaddress($addy, $convertBalance);
    $message = "Transaction: ".$doWithdrawal."<br>";
    //reset users balance to zero
    $updateBalance = "UPDATE users SET BALANCE = 0 WHERE USERID = '$userid'";
    $doUpdateBalance = mysqli_query($conn, $updateBalance);
    }
  }
}
```

13.8 Adding Game Features

At this point we technically have a functioning game, but we can still add things since we have a table in our database that keep track of all games played. Using this table we can build queries that are able to display player statistics to the user.

For example what if you wanted to display to the user the last 20 games they played?

First create the query:

```
$userStats = "SELECT * FROM games WHERE PLAYER = '$userid' ORDERBY GAMEID DESC LIMIT 20";
```

This will select the last 20 games in descending order where the PLAYER field matches the users' userid.

Then you can execute the query, and run it through a loop to output data.

```
while($dumpStats=mysqli_fetch_assoc($doUserStats))
      {
      echo $dumpStats['GAMEID'];
      echo $dumpStats['TARGET'];
      }
```

This is very sloppy, so let's put it into a table instead.

{222}
```
<table>
<tr>
<td>ID</td><td>TARGET</td><td>GUESS</td><td>WIN/LOSE</td>
</tr>
<?php
//user stats
$userStats = "SELECT * FROM games WHERE PLAYER = '$userid' ORDERBY GAMEID DESC LIMIT 20";
$doUserStats = mysqli_query($conn, $userStats);
  while($dumpStats=mysqli_fetch_assoc($doUserStats))
```

```php
    {
        echo "<tr>";
        echo "<td>".$dumpStats['GAMEID']."</td>";
        echo "<td>".$dumpStats['TARGET']."</td>";
        echo "<td>".$dumpStats['GUESS']."</td>";
        echo "<td>".$dumpStats['WINLOSE']."</td>";
        echo "</tr>";
    }
?>
</table>
```

Now it looks nicer, but since we are storing the user's guess and the win outcomes as integer's we will need to interpret these integers and make them into human readable outupts. For example users' guess of 1 doesn't mean anything to the user so we should have it output "Greater than 50" instead. We can do this with switch statements.

Create a new variable with the $dumpStats output for guess:

```php
$dumpGuess = $dumpStats['GUESS'];
```

Then add a switch statement for the three different possibilities.

```php
switch($dumpGuess){
        case 1:
        $guessOut = "Greater Than 50";
        break;
        case 2:
        $guessOut = "Less Than 50";
        break;
        case 3:
        $guessOut = "Exactly 50";
        break;
    }
```

You can do the same with the WINLOSE category as well.

```php
$dumpWin = $dumpStats['WINLOSE'];
    switch($dumpWin){
       case 0;
       $winLoseOut = "Win";
       break;
```

```
      case 1;
      $winLoseOut = "Lose";
      break;
   }
```

Together it would look something like this:

{223}
```
<table>
<tr>
<td>ID</td><td>TARGET</td><td>GUESS</td><td>WIN/LOSE</td>
</tr>
<?php
//user stats
$userStats = "SELECT * FROM games WHERE PLAYER = '$userid'
ORDERBY GAMEID DESC LIMIT 20";
$doUserStats - mysqli_query($conn, $userStats);
while($dumpStats=mysqli_fetch_assoc($doUserStats))
{
echo "<tr>";
echo "<td>".$dumpStats['GAMEID']."</td>";
echo "<td>".$dumpStats['TARGET']."</td>";
$dumpGuess = $dumpStats['GUESS'];
switch($dumpGuess){
   case 1:
   $guessOut = "Greater Than 50";
   break;
   case 2:
   $guessOut = "Less Than 50";
   break;
   case 3:
   $guessOut = "Exactly 50";
   break;
}
echo "<td>".$guessOut."</td>";
$dumpWin = $dumpStats['WINLOSE'];
switch($dumpWin){
   case 0:
   $winLoseOut = "Win";
   break;
   case 1:
   $winLoseOut = "Lose";
   break;
}
echo "<td>".$winLoseOut."</td>";
echo "</tr>";
}
?>
</table>
```

From here the rest is really up to you. Start building your own queries and see what features your can add.

Things you might want to try to add:

Every 1000 games the user receives a bonus.
Add a query that counts their total wins and losses.
Display the users win to lose ratio.

NOTES:

NOTES:

NOTES:

Made in the USA
Middletown, DE
10 June 2017